Whales and other sea
Mammals

Wild, Wild World of Animals

Whales &
Other Sea Mammals

A TIME-LIFE TELEVISION BOOK

Produced in Association with Vineyard Books, Inc.

Editor: Eleanor Graves
Series Editor: Charles Osborne
Senior Consultant: Lucille Ogle
Text Editor: Richard Oulahan
    Associate Text Editor: Bonnie Johnson
    Author: Thomas A. Dozier
    Assistant Editors: Peter Ainslie, Regina Grant Hersey
    Literary Research: Ellen Schachter
    Text Research: Nancy Levering
    Copy Editors: Robert J. Myer, Greg Weed
Picture Editor: Richard O. Pollard
    Picture Research: Judith Greene
    Permissions: Cecilia Waters
Book Designer and Art Director: Jos. Trautwein
    Art Assistant: Carl Van Brunt
Production Coordinator: Jane L. Quinson

WILD, WILD WORLD OF ANIMALS
TELEVISION PROGRAM
Producers: Jonathan Donald and Lothar Wolff
This Time-Life Television Book is published by Time-Life Films, Inc.
Bruce L. Paisner, *President*
J. Nicoll Durrie, *Business Manager*

Wild, Wild World of Animals

Whales &
Other Sea Mammals

Based on the television series
Wild, Wild World of Animals

Published by
TIME-LIFE FILMS

The excerpt from Moby Dick by Herman Melville is reprinted courtesy of The
Riverside Press.

The excerpt from The Living Sea by Jacques-Yves Cousteau with James
Dugan, copyright © 1963 by Harper & Row, Publishers, Inc., is reprinted by
permission of the publisher.

The excerpt from Scott's Last Expedition by R. F. Scott is reprinted courtesy
of John Murray (Publishers) Ltd.

The excerpt from De Bestiis marinis (Beasts of the Sea) by Georg Wilhelm
Steller is reprinted from Georg Wilhelm Steller: The Pioneer of Alaskan
Natural History by Leonard Stejneger, Harvard University Press, 1936,
courtesy of the publisher.

"The Seafarer's Tale" is reprinted from The Year of the Seal by Victor B.
Scheffer, copyright © 1970 by Victor B. Scheffer, courtesy of the author.

The excerpt from Lives of Game Animals by Ernest Thompson Seton,
copyright © 1925 by Ernest Thompson Seton, is reprinted by permission of
The Estate of Julia M. Seton.

ISBN 0-913948-10-1

Library of Congress Catalog Card Number: 76-45496

Printed in the United States of America.

Contents

INTRODUCTION

by Thomas A. Dozier 8

BALEEN WHALES 16

A selection from Moby Dick
by Herman Melville . . . 34

TOOTHED WHALES 40

DOLPHINS AND PORPOISES 46

A selection from The Living Sea
by Jacques-Yves Cousteau . . . 50

A selection from Scott's Last Expedition
by Robert Falcon Scott . . . 60

MANATEES AND DUGONGS 62

A selection from Beasts of the Sea
by Georg Wilhelm Steller . . . 68

SEALS, SEA LIONS AND WALRUSES 70

SEA OTTERS 100

A selection from Lives of Game Animals
by Ernest Thompson Seton . . . 108

SONGS AND SOUNDS FROM THE DEEP .. 110

STRUGGLE FOR SURVIVAL 116

BIBLIOGRAPHY AND CREDITS 126

INDEX 127

Introduction by Thomas A. Dozier

THE EARLIEST MAMMALS LIVED ON LAND, and most of them still do. But, starting perhaps 60 million years ago, several groups of four-footed land animals found it to their advantage to return to the sea in which they, and all living creatures, had had their beginnings. The reason for the retrocession was almost certainly the search for food. As provender became scarcer on land—perhaps due to some natural calamity such as ice shifting across the continents—the animals sought sustenance on the shores of the great oceans, at first probably scooping fish or other marine life from the water, taking gradually to the depths, all the while adapting their bodies in varying degrees to an aquatic existence. Nobody knows whose ancestor was the first to take the plunge, but naturalist Victor B. Scheffer, in his book *A Natural History of Marine Mammals*, has gone so far as to establish a chronological timetable or evolutionary calendar for the sea mammals. He believes that the four groups represent four distances in time from land ancestors and that the hands and feet of their members are a living clue to the distance. The sea otter as a marine mammal is, according to Scheffer, only 5 million years old. The pinnipeds (seals and walruses) are at least 30 million years old. The sirenians (manatees and dugongs) are at least 55 million years old and the cetaceans (whales and dolphins) at least 60 million years.

These are the marine mammals, four fascinating groups of about 118 species (out of a world total of more than 4,000 mammalian species) that live either entirely or mostly in the water, depend completely on food taken from the sea and have anatomical adaptations, such as flippers, fins and webbed feet, that equip them for life in the sea. They are not closely related within the phylum of mammals, and there are as many differences between species as there would be in a similar number of land mammals. The furry, four-foot-long sea otter is no more like the blubbery 100-foot blue whale (shown in the filmstrip at left) than a mouse is like an elephant. Nor does the bulbous, lethargic and slow-thinking manatee look or behave anything like the swift, playful and highly intelligent sea lion.

That they are true mammals there can be no doubt, for the warm-blooded sea creatures have all of the basic mammalian qualifications: a four-chambered heart, the ability of the female to bear live young and feed the offspring with milk produced in her own body and at least a few hairs somewhere on the skin. Of course, warm-bloodedness and the breathing of air through lungs are by no means exclusively mammalian traits, but they are taken for granted in mammals. (Unfortunately, nature is never completely precise in its definitions: The spiny anteater and the duck-billed platypus, both classified as mammals, are egg-layers, but both have hair and nurse their young.)

Among the marine mammals, the earthbound origins of the sea otter are self-evident, for it is only one of many species of the family of mustelids, all other members of which are basically terrestrial: river otters, weasels, badgers, skunks, martens and wolverines. Even within the otter family the sea otter is the only marine creature among 18 differing species, some of which live far from the sea in

Sea lion rookery, California

The vast array of marine mammals of the western hemisphere, all of which are drawn to scale in the chart at right, include pinnipeds (seals, sea lions and walruses), manatees, sea otters and whales. The largest creature among them—and in the world—is the mammoth 100-foot blue whale. Like all baleen whales, it feeds on krill, shrimplike creatures and other marine organisms drawn to one third their actual size in the circle in the center of the illustration. The toothed whales, such as the sperm whale in the lower right-hand corner of the chart, are not equipped to eat krill and feed instead on squid, as shown, as well as fish and cuttlefish. Although the seascape presented here is dominated by the great whales, their numbers have decreased so drastically that eight species—the right, bowhead, blue, sperm, humpback, fin, sei and gray whales—appear on the U.S. endangered species list. All the marine mammals represented, however, are protected in the United States by the Marine Mammal Protection Act of 1972.

10

BEARDED SEAL

COMMON DOLPHIN

HOODED SEAL

WALRUS

HARP SEAL AND PUP

HARBOR PORPOISE

RINGED SEAL

RIBBON SEAL

PILOT WHALE

CRABEATER SEAL

NARWHAL

BOWHEAD WHALE

LEOPARD SEAL

BELUGA WHALE

BAIR WHA

WEDDELL SEAL

PYGMY SPERM WHALE

SEI WHALE

All species on this chart are to scale

0   10   20   30   40   50   60

0   5   10   15

NORTHERN ELEPHANT SEAL

STELLER'S SEA LION

CALIFORNIA SEA LION

BOTTLENOSED DOLPHIN

GREY WHALE AND CALF

MANATEE

NORTHERN FUR SEALS

SEA OTTER

GREY SEAL

SPINNER DOLPHIN

PACIFIC WHITE-SIDED DOLPHIN

HAWAIIAN MONK SEAL

KILLER WHALE

DALL PORPOISE

MINKE WHALE

HARBOR SEAL

FALSE KILLER WHALE

Feeding on krill

ARCH-BEAKED WHALE

HUMPBACK WHALE

AKED

Krill

SPOTTED DOLPHIN

CUVIER'S BEAKED WHALE

NORTHERN RIGHT WHALE DOLPHIN

RISSO'S DOLPHIN

FIN WHALE

BLACK RIGHT WHALE

SPERM WHALE

BLUE WHALE

Feeding on giant squid

70   80   90   100 Feet

25   30 Meters

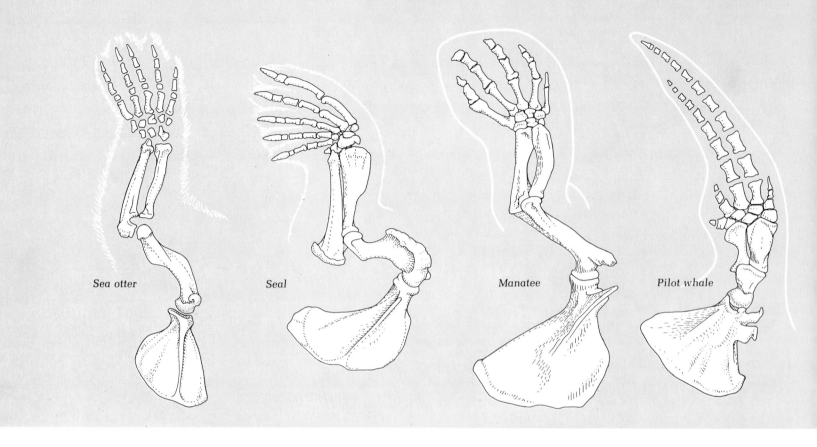

Sea otter   Seal   Manatee   Pilot whale

The drawing above, showing the skeletal forelimbs of four marine mammals, gives evidence of a terrestrial past, however distant, in each. The "hands" bear a remarkable resemblance to those of man, each having five jointed fingers, but, in the interest of streamlining, each marine mammal developed a "mitten" of fur or skin. The sea otter, the most recent aquatic convert, retains the most handlike appendage, which it uses for grasping food and tools. Among seals, which came to the water earlier, the arm is no longer a distinct limb, and the flipper is used for locomotion. Manatees, which evolved into marine mammals slightly earlier than seals, are completely aquatic, and their flippers are of relatively little use beyond steering and guiding food to their mouths. Whales, the oldest marine mammals, have stiff flippers whose only function is steering and, in certain species, slapping the water or a partner during mating.

high mountains, deserts and tropical forests. And, as the latest of the sea mammals to get in the swim, the sea otter is also the most amphibious. It dives, swims and floats on its back with complete ease but returns to the shore to give birth. On land, sea otters move about much less gracefully than some of the pinnipeds, the only other sea mammals with terrestrial ties.

The pinnipeds retain enough attachment to the land to indicate that their ancestors went from a terrestrial environment to a watery one more recently than the sirenians and whales. The oldest known pinniped remains are from the comparatively recent Miocene epoch, about 20 million years ago. Most scientists agree, however, that fossils of pinniped ancestors will eventually be found in deposits dating back to many millions of years earlier. Their anatomical similarities with modern land mammals—the retention of ears, conventional noses and divided rear flippers that can be used, however awkwardly, for land locomotion—are positive evidence of their terrestrial origins.

The manatee and dugong, the only surviving members of the sirenian order, represent a complete adaptation to the water and are unable to survive at all on land. Their hind limbs have disappeared entirely, but their forearms end in flippers and can be manipulated to handle food and hold their nursing young. There is little fossil evidence of the sirenians' land origins, although some scientists theorize that they have a common ancestor with the modern elephant of Africa and India. Some sirenians, as well as a few river dolphins, live in freshwater habitats.

Of all the marine mammals, the large and varied order of cetaceans is the farthest removed from the land and the most fishlike in appearance. There can be no doubt about their terrestrial origins, though. Newly formed whale fetuses are remarkably similar to those of land mammals: Four telltale limbs appear during early gestation, and, although the vestigial rear legs disappear before birth, the forelegs develop into flat flippers that retain the bone structure of a five-fingered hand. The fetal nostrils are first located at the end of the snout, but move to the top of the head before birth to become the whales' characteristic blowholes. The location of the blowholes enables the oceangoing giants to surface and breathe with minimum effort. Land animals are limited in growth potential by their body structure, but whales, buoyed to an almost weightless state by the water, have produced the largest creatures ever known. A newly born whale may be 25 feet long and weigh two tons.

Some cetologists believe that the baleen whales, which feed through a unique filtering system, have a different ancestral line from the other whale family, toothed whales. Others hold that all cetaceans have a common ancestor with ruminant ungulates like cows, goats and deer because of certain anatomical similarities such as multiple stomachs and extraordinarily long intestines.

Forrest G. Wood, in his book *Marine Mammals and Man*, noted that porpoises, like goats, rams and bulls, have a proclivity for butting and that they "are readily spooked, fleeing in a manner that may be analogous to a stampede." Wood points to other similarities between cetaceans and ungulates but admits that the case for a close kinship with the hoofed, herbivorous land animals is unproved, concluding: "For all that we know about them the porpoises and whales remain an enigmatic group whose early history still lies hidden in the remoteness of geologic time."

While the sea mammals move evolutionally deeper into their watery environments, other warm-blooded creatures are following them into the sea. Auks have double-purpose wings that can propel them equally well through the air and under the water. Penguins have abandoned the skies and their wings are useless except in the water. Among mammals, the most notable example of a land-dweller in the process of becoming a sea creature is the polar bear. Although it is indubitably a bear (in zoos it will hybridize with the brown bear species), it is an excellent swimmer and has oily, waterproof fur, a somewhat streamlined shape and forepaws that are half-webbed. These adaptations occurred because the polar bear lives in bleak Arctic regions where small animals, insects and suitable vegetation are less plentiful, so *Ursus maritimus* must take some of its food from the sea. It seems possible that if it continues to exist for a few million years, becoming more dependent on the sea, the polar bear may evolve into a sea mammal.

Despite differences in size and shape, the marine mammals (science has provided no Latin name for them as a group) possess certain common behavioral qualities. Although some are herbivorous and the rest carnivorous and some fight over mates and territory, they are generally peaceful and unaggressive animals, adopting toward all creatures but their natural prey a live-and-let-live attitude.

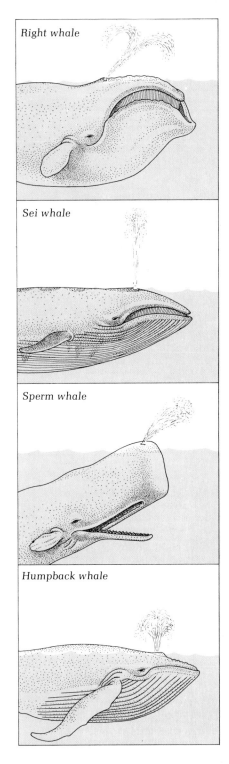

Right whale

Sei whale

Sperm whale

Humpback whale

The differences among the blows of four whales are shown above. The right whale has a V-shaped blow; the sei's is slender and conical. The blows of both the sperm and the humpback are pear-shaped, but the sperm's emerges at an angle of 45 degrees.

Most of the sea mammals are remarkably intelligent, especially the cetaceans, whose learning and reasoning abilities have so astounded investigators that some scientists are convinced that the cetacean brain is closer in capacity to that of man than any other animal's. Such a high level of intellectual ability, coupled with a friendly disposition, make the cetaceans among the most scientifically interesting and popular of all animals.

Sadly, all four groups share another common and disastrous characteristic: Their bodies are composed of materials that are commercially valuable to man. And man has not hesitated to kill off the sea mammals in appalling numbers. The aquatic air-breathers represent one of the most remarkable and successful migrations from one environment to another in all natural history—successful, that is, until man came along. Unless the human conscience conquers man's more savage and greedy instincts, the movement of the aquatic mammals from land to sea in search of survival and eventual perfection could turn out to be a move toward oblivion.

If extirpation at the hands of man is indeed to be the fate of the sea mammals, it will be ironic, for, even as he has slaughtered them, man has ambivalently been fascinated and awed by whales, dolphins, sea cows and the other warm-blooded creatures. That fascination, which sometimes amounted to reverence, has been amply reflected over the years in art, mythology, religion, music and literature. Around 3,000 B.C., an ancester of the aborigines of Australia painted on stone the accurate silhouette of a dolphin, one of the oldest known artistic representations of sea mammals. The legends of the sirens and the unicorn, the allegories of Jonah's ordeal in the belly of the "great fish" and of Captain Ahab's struggle with Moby Dick, the great white whale, all originated with the mammals that live in the sea. The crown prince of France was known as the dauphin, or dolphin, and the Delphic oracle of Greece was probably named for the same frolicsome creature. The ancient Greeks and the Phoenicians worshiped the dolphin as the "sacred fish." Small wonder that a long line of artists, led by that aboriginal painter of long ago, has immortalized the sea mammals in stone, bronze and oils and even on whalebone and the ivory tusks of walruses: the Cretan muralists, Raphael and other great masters, the scrimshaw artists of the 19th-century whaling fleets.

Writers from Aristotle to Melville have celebrated the whale. Columbus and Henry Hudson wrote solemnly of encounters with mermaids, which were actually either manatees or seals, on their voyages of discovery, and Hans Christian Andersen concocted a classic fairy tale about a little mermaid who made a tragic decision to leave the sea—for the love of a man. Such tales and fancies are perhaps the most poignant reminders of the paradox that these groups of animals, which for centuries have fired man's imagination, should have been brought, by man, to the very edge of extinction.

Gray whale in Scammon Lagoon

Baleen Whales

Alone among the warm-blooded, air-breathing mammals that have returned to the sea after an evolutionary period on the land, only whales have severed virtually all connections with their terrestrial past. When washed up on a beach or stranded in shoal water they are completely immobilized and die quickly from dehydration or the crushing weight of their own bodies. But neither can they exist for long in the ocean's depths, since they must surface periodically to breathe. They have thus evolved as creatures whose permanent habitat can be neither the deeps of the ocean where the fish swim, nor the earth where fellow mammals crawl, nor the air where birds fly but rather the zone where sea and sky meet. This is the whale's domain.

In the process of their unique evolution, whales—or cetaceans, as they are called scientifically—have developed characteristics that are common to all 78 species of their order: torpedo-shaped bodies, horizontal tail flukes, front limbs that have evolved into flippers, no external ears, and breathing holes that are set flush in the tops of their heads. Otherwise these great mammals differ dramatically in appearance, color and size.

One major difference divides the order Cetacea into two distinct suborders: Odontoceti, the toothed whales, and Mysticeti, or baleen whales. The baleens, constituting three families—six kinds of rorquals, or finback whales, gray whales and right whales—differ most strikingly from their cousins in their great size and in the interior design of their mouths. Instead of teeth, the mouths of baleen whales are filled with as many as 400 thin, flexible plates on each side of the jaw through which they filter seawater to strain out the tiny plankton and crustaceans (collectively called krill) that are their basic diet. These odd strainers, the baleen, are known commercially as whalebone and were once used for the constraining stays of Victorian corsets.

Despite their lack of true teeth and their dainty diet, the baleens number in their group all but one of the largest cetaceans (among toothed whales, only the sperm whale is in the baleens' heavyweight class). The largest of the baleens, the great blue whale, is the biggest animal that ever existed. While the blue's average adult length is 80 to 90 feet, specimens of about 100 feet have been repeatedly sighted. The largest accurately measured blue whale on record was an enormous female, caught in the waters near Antarctica in 1931. It measured 96 feet, eight inches from the point of the upper jaw to the notch of the tail fluke.

Based on piecemeal weighings, the estimated weight of the giantess was 392,000 pounds, the equivalent of 130 compact station wagons or 2,240 men.

The blue is the largest member of the rorqual family, a group of comparably sized whales that also includes four other species—the fin whale or common rorqual; the sei; Bryde's rorqual; and the minke (also called the piked or lesser rorqual). The family name is derived from the Norwegian words for "tubed whale" and describes the distinctive pleats that line the undersides of all rorquals from the underslung lower jaw to the midsection. The only other whale with similar striated markings is the closely related humpback whale. Its silhouette is much less sleek than the streamlined shape of true rorquals.

Until the adoption of modern whaling techniques and equipment, the rorquals were relatively safe from man because they were too big to approach in small boats and usually fast enough to escape hand-hurled harpoons. On the infrequent occasions when they were killed, they often frustrated the hunters by sinking quickly and sometimes swamping the whaleboats. Technology stripped the rorqual's last defenses away: the introduction of explosive harpoons, fast whale-hunting motorboats, factory ships to process blubber and other whale products on an assembly-line basis and air-injecting apparatus that made it possible to float a whale carcass alongside a ship and haul it for great distances. Since an average blue whale can furnish about 120 barrels of high-grade oil, the blues became prime targets, and their population declined drastically. In the 1930–31 whaling season the worldwide catch was 29,649 blues. By the 1964–65 season all the whalers of the world could find only 372 blues to kill.

The gray whale, the lone species of a baleen family of the same name, has also been slaughtered almost to the point of extinction, and in fact the Atlantic species is extinct. But it has made a comeback in the Pacific as a result of recent conservation efforts.

The right whales, the third family of baleens, which include several subspecies, are not nearly so big and handsome as the blue and the gray. This species was the favorite of early whalers because it was relatively slow and easily harpooned, floated when killed and could be sliced up with comparative ease. It got its name from such characteristics: It was the "right" whale to go after. As a result it was almost extinct by the end of the last century.

Southern right whale

The Enduring Rights

Hunted since the 11th century, four of the five species of right whales have been slaughtered nearly out of existence, and one species—the Greenland, or bowhead, whale—has become the rarest of all whales. The fifth species, the pygmy right whale, has never been numerous enough to warrant commercial exploitation. Because they are lethargic swimmers that conveniently float when dead, right whales were natural targets for early whalers in their relatively small and primitive boats. But when a British whaling expedition in 1912 failed to turn up a single bowhead in a North Atlantic area in which they had once abounded, right whales were largely abandoned in favor of a more accessible species.

Occasional sightings in the Bering Sea and Hudson Bay in recent years have puzzled cetologists, who are at a loss to explain why the species, left unmolested for so long, has neither staged a more successful comeback nor died out completely. The discovery about 15 years ago of a herd of southern right whales, like the one pictured below, which gather each year in the waters off Patagonia in Argentina, gave support to hopes that the species would recover. These hopes were further buoyed in 1974 when part of the area was set aside as a permanent sanctuary for the animals, partly as a result of the efforts of the New York Zoological Society.

Right whales are massive creatures up to 55 feet long and often nearly as big in girth. The head accounts for perhaps a third of the body length and is equipped with a grotesquely curving mouth with baleen 14 feet long hanging fringelike from the upper jaw.

RICHARD ELLIS-1974

The right whales shown above are from a series of whale paintings by Richard Ellis, three of which are included in this book. Right whales are equipped with peculiar thick, tough, white growths called callosities covering their otherwise soft skin. Callosities are a boon to cetologists in identifying individuals because they form a unique pattern on each whale. The largest area of growth is on the whale's head and was called a "bonnet" by early whalers. Dr. Roger Payne, research zoologist with the New York Zoological Society, believes that the callosities function as a splash guard for the blowhole in breaching whales. In rare aggressive displays—usually between two or more males vying for the same female—the growths can cause abrasions when scraped against a competitor's sensitive skin.

19

Whale of a Tail

The power of a cetacean's tail, dramatically evident in the picture at left, is expended through two lobes called flukes, which, with the vertical movement of the tail, propel the animals through the water and act as rudders. Working much like a frogman's legs and flippers, the flukes beat vertically in the water, bending at a pivot at the base of the tail.

Cetologists have been amused to learn that southern right whales in a playful mood sometimes use their flukes to "sail." Body submerged, the whale elevates its flukes above the surface at a right angle to the wind, which pushes the animal along and establishes it as the only known marine life—other than certain jellyfish—to use wind for propulsion. Such activity may go on for three or four hours, with the whales frolicking in a variety of games, turning their flukes this way and that to catch the wind.

Whales also use their flukes in another activity, called lobtailing, which scientists also originally regarded as playful behavior. Raising its flukes high above the water, a whale will bring them down with a thunderous crash, repeating the maneuver over and over. One whale's lobtailing often serves as a cue to others nearby and is likely to set off a mass display of raw power. When Dr. Payne, who has studied the right whales of Patagonia extensively, realized that lobtailing often followed an increase in wind, he theorized that it may be some sort of whale communication. High winds create underwater noise that interferes with whales' low-frequency "speech" (see pages 112–113). Lobtailing may be a means of overcoming that interference so that members of a herd can stay together, even in the worst of storms.

Flukes stretching some 20 feet across, a southern right whale off Patagonia lifts its tail in preparation for a dive (left). Whales frequently suspend themselves vertically in the water with flukes aloft, coming up for breath every 20 minutes or so instead of the usual two or three. Scientists speculate that whales in this position are resting, though they have also observed female whales doing the same thing in an apparent effort to avoid mating.

The Tiny Food of Giants

Whalebone, once used in corsets, skirt hoops, umbrellas and riding crops, isn't really bone at all. It is baleen, a flexible, fingernaillike substance that grows in long, narrow strips from the upper jaw of baleen whales. Fringed with tiny bristles, the baleen serves as a giant strainer to trap krill, tiny shrimplike organisms, worms, snails and other drifting creatures that are part of the abundant supply of oceanic plankton. It is primarily on these tiny creatures that many of the leviathans of the ocean are nourished.

Right whales, like the southern right below, ingest tons of krill by swimming openmouthed through shoals of it in the ocean's colder waters, where krill is most abundant. As they swim they filter millions of gallons of water through their baleen. Scientists are uncertain how krill moves from baleen to throat but speculate that mouth muscles force out seawater and that a swipe across the baleen with the mammoth whale tongue dislodges the krill.

As the photographs on the opposite page show, krill comes in a variety of colorful shapes and sizes, depending largely on its origin—Arctic or Antarctic.

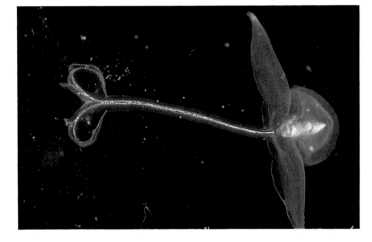

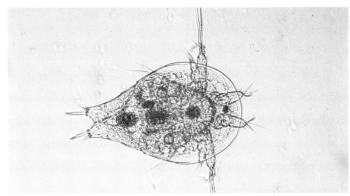

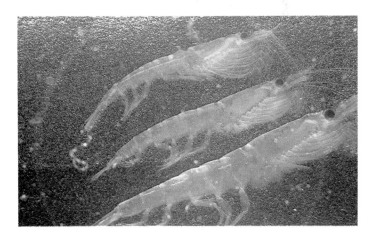

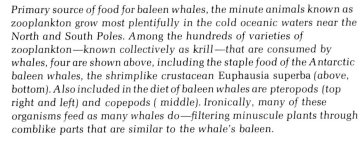

Primary source of food for baleen whales, the minute animals known as zooplankton grow most plentifully in the cold oceanic waters near the North and South Poles. Among the hundreds of varieties of zooplankton—known collectively as krill—that are consumed by whales, four are shown above, including the staple food of the Antarctic baleen whales, the shrimplike crustacean Euphausia superba (above, bottom). Also included in the diet of baleen whales are pteropods (top right and left) and copepods (middle). Ironically, many of these organisms feed as many whales do—filtering minuscule plants through comblike parts that are similar to the whale's baleen.

Blue Behemoths

Although it was not hunted seriously until a hundred years ago, the blue whale has been slaughtered in such quantity that it has been reduced to perhaps 6 percent of its former numbers. Its future was so precarious that in 1966 it was afforded complete, worldwide protection by the International Whaling Commission.

Traveling alone, in pairs or in small family groups, blue whales migrate south to calve and mate in the winter, fasting in the temperate or tropical waters and losing considerable weight en route to the breeding areas. Baby blues are born after an 11-month gestation and are almost 25 feet long at birth. They grow at an astounding rate, doubling their weight the first week of life and gaining some 200 pounds a day thereafter. By the time they are weaned, at the age of seven months, they are around 50 feet long and weigh approximately 23 tons.

Blue whales are a cosmopolitan breed, ranging through all the oceans to the ice packs at both poles. It is because they are so fragmented and widely separated that they may never recover from the whaling industry's plunder.

Blue whales, sometimes known as sulphur bottoms because of yellowish algae that bloom on their skin, are swift, powerful swimmers that cruise at speeds of 10 to 12 miles per hour and swim even faster if necessary. One blue was clocked at 23 miles per hour for a period of 10 minutes, and another harpooned specimen once dragged a 90-foot whaling boat, its engines revved full-speed astern, for 50 miles—a trip that took seven hours—before it died. Blue whales in the northern hemisphere are generally smaller than those in the southern, although "pygmy" blues have been observed in the southern Indian Ocean.

Gray Migrants of the Pacific

Three different populations of gray whales once existed in great numbers in the western and eastern Pacific and in the North Atlantic. Today only the eastern Pacific group survives; the others were the victims of whaling overkills. The remaining grays were on the brink of extinction, reduced to possibly no more than 250 individuals, when rigid protection laws were enacted in 1946. Today there are an estimated 12,000 grays.

Each year the slow-moving whales make a lengthy migration from their summer habitat in the Bering Sea to shallow lagoons on the coast of Baja California (shown on page 15), where they give birth and breed. Female grays are such ferocious defenders of their young that they were sometimes called devilfish. Because of the large accumulations of barnacles on their skin—more than on any other cetacean—grays have also been called mossback whales.

Clowning in the Kelp

Alone or in small groups, gray whales generally fast during their four- to six-thousand-mile annual migration to the nuptial lagoons of Baja California. The journey takes about four months of round-the-clock swimming, the whales cruising at four miles per hour.

But the female gray on these pages inexplicably interrupted her trek for an entire day to swim and cavort among the kelp beds (below) off Point Loma, California, before continuing south.

Gray whales were hunted intensively off southern California during the mid-19th century. Charles Scammon, a whaling captain who discovered the gray's breeding grounds, wrote at the time in his diary: "In the seasons of 1858 and 1859, not only the bays and lagoons were teeming [with whalers] but the outside coast was lined with ships, from San Diego southward to Cape St. Lucas." Though the gray whale has recovered somewhat from such exploitation, a steady stream of whale-watchers cruising the lagoons in power boats has more recently created considerable disturbance among the species.

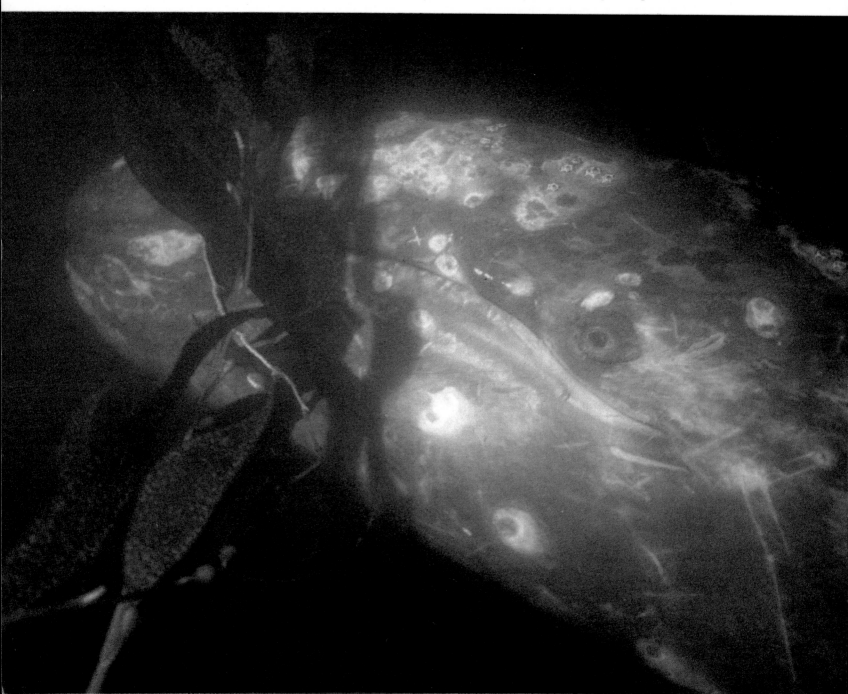

A female gray whale breaches, wearing an outrageous bonnet of kelp.
Many kinds of whales love to play among kelp beds, lying on their sides
and patting the kelp with their flippers, or draping it over their heads and
then swimming forward while the green strands slide down their bodies.
The gray on these pages was in a particularly friendly mood and allowed
the photographer to pat her and swim alongside for much of the day.

The Humpback Whale

The humpback whale is a slow, chunky creature up to 50 feet long and perhaps 40 feet around. It is among the slowest of whales, swimming from two to five miles per hour, with a top speed of nine miles per hour when pursued.

The humpback is essentially a coastal inhabitant, frequently entering harbors and even venturing up the mouths of large rivers. That fact, along with its leisurely movement, has made it an exceedingly vulnerable target. Though it has been protected by the International Whaling Commission since 1966, the humpback is still considered a rare and endangered species. It survives in three distinct populations—the North Atlantic, the North Pacific and the southern hemisphere—but only in the North Atlantic has it shown signs of recovery.

The humpback isn't really humpbacked at all but gets its name from its habit of exposing a large area of its back when it dives, giving it a hunched appearance. It also "flukes" when diving (below), elevating its tail above the water and displaying the distinctive serrations it bears on the trailing edges of its flukes.

The humpback is equipped with extraordinary white flippers that extend up to 15 feet from its sides. The whale has a playful habit of slapping the water—or, in the case of mating humpbacks, its partner—with its flippers, producing a sound that can be heard miles away.

31

In spite of its slowness, the humpback is considered the most athletic of whales, known among cetologists for its antic behavior. Leaping high into the air, it crashes on its back into the water or sometimes turns complete somersaults in midair. Humpbacks are hosts to vast colonies of parasites. A single whale may be burdened with as much as a half ton of barnacles. Some whalemen believe that the whale's prodigious leaps may be efforts to get rid of the irritating pests.

33

MOBY DICK

by Herman Melville

Moby Dick, the great white whale of Melville's classic novel, attacked whaling boats with such malevolent intelligence that his very name struck awe and fear among New England mariners. This excerpt from the final episode of Moby Dick, *illustrated with Rockwell Kent's drawings, recounts the three-day battle that was the ultimate confrontation between the whale and its obsessed pursuer, Captain Ahab.*

A whole hour now passed; gold-beaten out to ages. Time itself now held long breaths with keen suspense. But at last, some three points off the weather bow, Ahab descried the spout again, and instantly from the three mast-heads three shrieks went up as if the tongues of fire had voiced it.

"Forehead to forehead I meet thee, this third time, Moby Dick! On deck there!—brace sharper up; crowd her into the wind's eye. He's too far off to lower yet, Mr. Starbuck. The sails shake! Stand over that helmsman with a top-maul! So, so; he travels fast, and I must down. But let me have one more good round look aloft here at the sea; there's time for that. An old, old sight, and yet somehow so young; aye, and not changed a wink since I first saw it, a boy, from the sand-hills of Nantucket! The same!—the same!—the same to Noah as to me. There's a soft shower to leeward. Such lovely leewardings! They must lead somewhere—to something else than common land, more palmy than the palms. Leeward! the white whale goes that way; look to windward, then; the better if the bitterer quarter. But good bye, good bye, old mast-head! What's this?—green? aye, tiny mosses in these warped cracks. No such green weather stains on Ahab's head! There's the difference now between man's old age and matter's. But aye, old mast, we both grow old together; sound in our hulls, though, are we not, my ship? Aye, minus a leg, that's all. By heaven this dead wood has the better of my live flesh every way. I can't compare with it; and I've known some ships made of dead trees outlast the lives of men made of the most vital stuff of vital fathers. What's that he said? he should still go before me, my pilot; and yet to be seen again? But where? Will I have eyes at the bottom of the sea, supposing I descend those endless stairs? and all night I've been sailing from him, wherever he did sink to. Aye, aye, like many more thou told'st direful truth as touching thyself, O Parsee; but, Ahab, there thy shot fell short. Good by, mast-head—keep a good eye upon the whale, the while I'm gone. We'll talk to-morrow, nay, to-night, when the white whale lies down there, tied by head and tail."

He gave the word; and still gazing round him, was steadily lowered through the cloven blue air to the deck.

In due time the boats were lowered; but as standing in his shallop's stern, Ahab just hovered upon the point of the descent, he waved to the mate,—who held one of the tackle-ropes on deck—and bade him pause.

"Starbuck!"

"Sir?"

"For the third time my soul's ship starts upon this voyage, Starbuck."

"Aye, sir, thou wilt have it so."

"Some ships sail from their ports, and ever afterwards are missing, Starbuck!"

"Truth, sir: saddest truth."

"Some men die at ebb tide; some at low water; some at the full of the flood;—and I feel now like a billow that's all one crested comb, Starbuck. I am old—shake hands with me, man."

Their hands met; their eyes fastened; Starbuck's tears the glue.

"Oh, my captain, my captain!—noble heart—go

not—go not!—see, it's a brave man that weeps; how great the agony of the persuasion then!"

"Lower away!"—cried Ahab, tossing the mate's arm from him. "Stand by the crew!"

In an instant the boat was pulling round close under the stern. "The sharks! the sharks!" cried a voice from the low cabin-window there; "O master, my master, come back!"

But Ahab heard nothing; for his own voice was high-lifted then; and the boat leaped on.

Yet the voice spake true; for scarce had he pushed from the ship, when numbers of sharks, seemingly rising from out the dark waters beneath the hull, maliciously snapped at the blades of the oars, every time they dipped in the water; and in this way accompanied the boat with their bites. It is a thing not uncommonly happening to the whale-boats in those swarming seas; the sharks at times apparently following them in the same prescient way that vultures hover over the banners of marching regiments in the east. But these were the first sharks that had been observed by the Pequod since the White Whale had been first descried; and whether it was that Ahab's crew were all such tiger-yellow barbarians, and therefore their flesh more musky to the senses of the sharks—a matter some-times well known to affect them,—however it was, they seemed to follow that one boat without molesting the others.

"Heart of wrought steel!" murmured Starbuck gazing over the side, and following with his eyes the receding boat—"canst thou yet ring boldly to that sight?—lowering thy keel among ravening sharks, and followed by them, open-mouthed to the chase; and this the critical third day?—For when three days flow together in one continuous pursuit; be sure the first is the morning, the second the noon, and the third the evening and the end of that thing—be that end what it may. Oh! my God! what is this that shoots through me, and leaves me so deadly calm yet expectant,—fixed at the top of a shudder! Future things swim before me, as in empty outlines and skeletons; all the past is somehow grown dim. Mary, girl! thou fadest in pale glories behind me; boy! I seem to see but thy eyes grown wondrous blue. Strangest problems of life seem clearing; but clouds sweep between—Is my journey's end coming? My legs feel faint; like his who has footed it all day. Feel thy heart,—beats it yet?—Stir thyself,

Starbuck!—stave it off—move, move! speak aloud!—Mast-head there! See ye my boy's hand on the hill?—Crazed;—aloft there!—keep thy keenest eye upon the boats:—mark well the whale!—Ho! again!—drive off that hawk! see! he pecks—he tears the vane"—pointing to the red flag flying at the main-truck—"Ha! he soars away with it!—Where's the old man now? see'st thou that sight, oh Ahab!—shudder, shudder!"

The boats had not gone very far, when by a signal from the mast-heads—a downward pointed arm, Ahab knew that the whale had sounded; but intending to be near him at the next rising, he held on his way a little sideways from the vessel; the becharmed crew maintaining the profound-est silence, as the head-beat waves hammered and ham-mered against the opposing bow.

"Drive, drive in your nails, oh ye waves! to their utter-most heads drive them in! ye but strike a thing without a lid; and no coffin and no hearse can be mine:—and hemp only can kill me! Ha! ha!"

Suddenly the waters around them slowly swelled in broad circles; then quickly upheaved, as if sideways sliding from a submerged berg of ice, swiftly rising to the surface. A low rumbling sound was heard; a subterraneous hum; and then all held their breaths; as bedraggled with trailing ropes, and harpoons, and lances, a vast form shot lengthwise, but obliquely from the sea. Shrouded in a thin drooping veil of mist, it hovered for a moment in the rainbowed air; and then fell swamping back into the deep. Crushed thirty feet upwards, the waters flashed for an instant like heaps of fountains, then brokenly sank in a shower of flakes, leaving the circling surface creamed like new milk around the marble trunk of the whale.

"Give way!" cried Ahab to the oarsmen, and the boats darted forward to the attack; but maddened by yesterday's fresh irons that corroded in him, Moby Dick seemed combinedly possessed by all the angels that fell from heaven. The wide tiers of welded tendons overspreading his broad white forehead, beneath the transparent skin, looked knitted together; as head on, he came churning his tail among the boats, and once more flailed them apart; spilling out the irons and lances from the two mates' boats, and dashing in one side of the upper part of their bows, but leaving Ahab's almost without a scar.

While Daggoo and Queequeg were stopping the strained planks; and as the whale swimming out from them, turned, and showed one entire flank as he shot by them again; at that moment a quick cry went up. Lashed round and round to the fish's back; pinioned in the turns in which, during the past night, the whale had reeled the involutions of the lines around him, the half torn body of the Parsee was seen; his sable raiment frayed to shreds; his distended eyes turned full upon old Ahab.

The harpoon dropped from his hand.

"Befooled, befooled!"—drawing in a long lean breath—"Aye, Parsee! I see thee again.—Aye, and thou goest before; and this, *this* then is the hearse that thou didst promise. But I hold thee to the last letter of thy word. Where is the second hearse? Away, mates, to the ship!

36

those boats are useless now; repair them if ye can in time, and return to me; if not, Ahab is enough to die—Down, men! the first thing that but offers to jump from this boat I stand in, that thing I harpoon. Ye are not other men, but my arms and my legs; and so obey me.—Where's the whale? gone down again?"

But he looked too nigh the boat; for as if bent upon escaping with the corpse he bore, and as if the particular place of the last encounter had been but a stage in his leeward voyage, Moby Dick was now again steadily swimming forward; and had almost passed the ship,— which thus far had been sailing in the contrary direction to him, though for the present her headway had been stopped. He seemed swimming with his utmost velocity, and now only intent upon pursuing his own straight path in the sea.

"Oh! Ahab," cried Starbuck, "not too late is it, even now, the third day, to desist. See! Moby Dick seeks thee not. It is thou, thou, that madly seekest him!"

Setting sail to the rising wind, the lonely boat was swiftly impelled to leeward, by both oars and canvas. And at last when Ahab was sliding by the vessel, so near as plainly to distinguish Starbuck's face as he leaned over the rail, he hailed him to turn the vessel about, and follow him, not too swiftly, at a judicious interval. Glancing upwards, he saw Tashtego, Queequeg, and Daggoo, eagerly mounting to the three mast-heads; while the oarsmen were rocking in the two staved boats which had just been hoisted to the side, and were busily at work in repairing them. One after the other, through the portholes, as he sped, he also caught flying glimpses of Stubb and Flask, busying themselves on deck among bundles of new irons and lances. As he saw all this; as he heard the hammers in the broken boats; far other hammers seemed driving a nail into his heart. But he rallied. And now marking that the vane or flag was gone from the mainmast-head, he shouted to Tashtego, who had just gained that perch, to descend again for another flag, and a hammer and nails, and so nail it to the mast.

Whether fagged by the three days' running chase, and the resistance to his swimming in the knotted hamper he bore; or whether it was some latent deceitfulness and malice in him: whichever was true, the White Whale's way now began to abate, as it seemed, from the boat so rapidly nearing him once more; though indeed the whale's last start had not been so long a one as before. And still as Ahab glided over the waves the unpitying sharks accompanied him; and so pertinaciously stuck to the boat; and so continually bit at the plying oars, that the blades became jagged and crunched, and left small splinters in the sea, at almost every dip.

"Heed them not! those teeth but give new rowlocks to your oars. Pull on! 'tis the better rest, the shark's jaw than the yielding water."

"But at every bite, sir, the thin blades grow smaller and smaller!"

"They will last long enough! pull on!—But who can tell"—he muttered—"whether these sharks swim to feast on the whale or on Ahab?—But pull on! Aye, all alive, now—we near him. The helm! take the helm; let me pass,"—and so saying, two of the oarsmen helped him forward to the bows of the still flying boat.

At length as the craft was cast to one side, and ran ranging along with the White Whale's flank, he seemed strangely oblivious of its advance—as the whale sometimes will—and Ahab was fairly within the smoky mountain mist, which, thrown off from the whale's spout, curled round his great, Monadnock hump; he was even thus close to him; when, with body arched back, and both arms lengthwise high-lifted to the poise, he darted his fierce iron, and his far fiercer curse into the hated whale. As both steel and curse sank to the socket, as if sucked into a morass, Moby Dick sideways writhed; spasmodically rolled his nigh flank against the bow, and, without staving a hole in it, so suddenly canted the boat over, that had it not been for the elevated part of the gunwale to which he then clung, Ahab would once more have been tossed into the sea. As it was, three of the oarsmen—who foreknew not the precise instant of the dart, and were therefore unprepared for its effects—these were flung out; but so fell, that, in an instant two of them clutched the gunwale again, and rising to its level on a combing wave, hurled

themselves bodily inboard again; the third man helplessly dropping astern, but still afloat and swimming.

Almost simultaneously, with a mighty volition of ungraduated, instantaneous swiftness, the White Whale darted through the weltering sea. But when Ahab cried out to the steersman to take new turns with the line, and hold it so; and commanded the crew to turn round on their seats, and tow the boat up to the mark; the moment the treacherous line felt that double strain and tug, it snapped in the empty air!

"What breaks in me? Some sinew cracks!—'tis whole again; oars! oars! Burst in upon him!"

Hearing the tremendous rush of the sea-crashing boat, the whale wheeled round to present his blank forehead at bay; but in that evolution, catching sight of the nearing black hull of the ship; seemingly seeing in it the source of all his persecutions; bethinking it—it may be—a larger and nobler foe; of a sudden, he bore down upon its advancing prow, smiting his jaws amid fiery showers of foam.

Ahab staggered; his hand smote his forehead. "I grow blind; hands! stretch out before me that I may yet grope my way. Is't night?"

"The whale! The ship!" cried the cringing oarsmen.

"Oars! oars! Slope downwards to thy depths, O sea, that ere it be for ever too late, Ahab may slide this last, last time upon his mark! I see: the ship! the ship! Dash on, my men! Will ye not save my ship?"

But as the oarsmen violently forced their boat through the sledge-hammering seas, the before whale-smitten bow-ends of two planks burst through, and in an instant almost, the temporarily disabled boat lay nearly level with the waves; its half-wading, splashing crew, trying hard to stop the gap and bale out the pouring water.

Meantime, for that one beholding instant, Tashtego's mast-head hammer remained suspended in his hand; and the red flag, half-wrapping him as with a plaid, then streamed itself straight out from him, as his own forward-flowing heart; while Starbuck and Stubb, standing upon the bowsprit beneath, caught sight of the down-coming monster just as soon as he.

"The whale, the whale! Up helm; up helm! Oh, all ye sweet powers of air, now hug me close! Let not Starbuck die, if die he must, in a woman's fainting fit. Up helm, I say—ye fools, the jaw! the jaw! Is this the end of all my bursting prayers? all my life-long fidelities? Oh, Ahab, Ahab, lo, thy work. Steady! helmsman, steady. Nay, nay! Up helm again! He turns to meet us! Oh, his unappeasable brow drives on towards one, whose duty tells him he cannot depart. My God, stand by me now!"

"Stand not by me, but stand under me, whoever you are that will now help Stubb; for Stubb, too, sticks here. I grin at thee, thou grinning whale! Who ever helped Stubb, or kept Stubb awake, but Stubb's own unwinking eye? And now poor Stubb goes to bed upon a mattrass that is all too soft; would it were stuffed with brushwood! I grin at thee, thou grinning whale! Look ye, sun, moon, and stars! I call

38

ye assassins of as good a fellow as ever spouted up his ghost. For all that, I would yet ring glasses with ye, would ye but hand the cup! Oh, oh! oh, oh! thou grinning whale, but there'll be plenty of gulping soon! Why fly ye not, O Ahab! For me, off shoes and jacket to it; let Stubb die in his drawers! A most mouldy and over salted death, though;—cherries! cherries! cherries! Oh, Flask, for one red cherry ere we die!"

"Cherries? I only wish that we were where they grow. Oh, Stubb, I hope my poor mother's drawn my part-pay ere this; if not, few coppers will now come to her, for the voyage is up."

From the ship's bows, nearly all the seamen now hung inactive; hammers, bits of plank, lances and harpoons, mechanically retained in their hands, just as they had darted from their various employments; all their enchanted eyes intent upon the whale, which from side to side strangely vibrating his predestinating head, sent a broad band of overspreading semicircular foam before him as he rushed. Retribution, swift vengeance, eternal malice were in his whole aspect, and spite of all that mortal man could do, the solid white buttress of his forehead smote the ship's starboard bow, till men and timbers reeled. Some fell flat upon their faces. Like dislodged trucks, the heads of the harpooneers aloft shook on their bull-like necks. Through the breach, they heard the waters pour, as mountain torrents down a flume.

"The ship! The hearse!—the second hearse!" cried Ahab from the boat; "its wood could only be American!"

Diving beneath the settling ship, the whale ran quivering along its keel; but turning under water, swiftly shot to the surface again, far off the other bow, but within a few yards of Ahab's boat, where, for a time, he lay quiescent.

"I turn my body from the sun. What ho, Tashtego! let me hear thy hammer. Oh! ye three unsurrendered spires of mine; thou uncracked keel; and only god-bullied hull; thou firm deck, and haughty helm, and Pole-pointed prow,—death-glorious ship! must ye then perish, and without me? Am I cut off from the last fond pride of meanest shipwrecked captains? Oh, lonely death on lonely life! Oh, now I feel my topmost greatness lies in my topmost grief. Ho, ho! from all your furthest bounds, pour ye now in, ye bold billows of my whole foregone life, and top this one piled comber of my death! Towards thee I roll, thou all-destroying but unconquering whale; to the last I grapple with thee; from the hell's heart I stab at thee; for hate's sake I spit my last breath at thee. Sink all coffins and all hearses to one common pool! and since neither can be mine, let me then tow to pieces, while still chasing thee, though tied to thee, thou damned whale! *Thus,* I give up the spear!"

The harpoon was darted; the stricken whale flew forward; with igniting velocity the line ran through the groove;—ran foul. Ahab stooped to clear it; he did clear it; but the flying turn caught him round the neck, and voicelessly as Turkish mutes bowstring their victim, he was shot out of the boat, ere the crew knew he was gone. Next instant, the heavy eye-splice in the rope's final end flew out of the stark-empty tub, knocked down an oarsman, and smiting the sea, disappeared in its depths.

For an instant, the tranced boat's crew stood still; then turned. "The ship? Great God, where is the ship?" Soon they through dim, bewildering mediums saw her sidelong fading phantom, as in the gaseous Fata Morgana; only the uppermost masts out of water; while fixed by infatuation, or fidelity, or fate, to their once lofty perches, the pagan harpooneers still maintained their sinking lookouts on the sea. And now, concentric circles seized the lone boat itself, and all its crew, and each floating oar, and every lance-pole, and spinning, animate and inanimate, all round and round in one vortex, carried the smallest chip of the Pequod out of sight.

But as the last whelmings intermixingly poured themselves over the sunken head of the Indian at the mainmast, leaving a few inches of the erect spar yet visible, together with long streaming yards of the flag, which calmly undulated, with ironical coincidings, over the destroying billows they almost touched;—at that instant, a red arm and a hammer hovered backwardly uplifted in the open air, in the act of nailing the flag faster and yet faster to the subsiding spar. A sky-hawk that tauntingly had followed the main-truck downwards from its natural home among

the stars, pecking at the flag, and incommoding Tashtego there; this bird now chanced to intercept its broad fluttering wing between the hammer and the wood; and simultaneously feeling that etherial thrill, the submerged savage beneath, in his death-gasp, kept his hammer frozen there; and so the bird of heaven, with archangelic shrieks, and his imperial beak thrust upwards, and his whole captive form folded in the flag of Ahab, went down with his ship, which, like Satan, would not sink to hell till she had dragged a living part of heaven along with her, and helmeted herself with it.

Now small fowls flew screaming over the yet yawning gulf; a sullen white surf beat against its steep sides; then all collapsed, and the great shroud of the sea rolled on as it rolled five thousand years ago.

Toothed Whales

Six whale families in a bewildering array of shapes, sizes and colors constitute the suborder Odontoceti, or toothed whales. The giant of the tribe is the enormous sperm whale, or cachalot, the third largest creature on earth, close behind the blue and fin whales. The middleweights of the toothed tribe are the beautiful white, or beluga, whale; the bizarre narwhal, with its unicornlike tusk; and the bottle-nosed and beaked whales, which are identified by their distinctive profiles. Smallest and most numerous members of the suborder are the porpoises and the dolphins. Although they are true whales, they are classified separately as delphinids (see page 46).

Teeth are the common denominator, but the Odontoceti are equipped with almost as many different arrangements of teeth as there are families in the suborder. Some, like the sperms, have teeth only in their lower jaws; others, such as the narwhals, have just two teeth in the upper jaw; and some delphinids have 200 or more tiny, sharp teeth. The Layard's, or strap-toothed, whale, a beaked whale, is equipped with a pair of lower tusks that curve up like scimitars over its snout and block its lower jaw from opening beyond a certain point.

The sperm whale is easily the best known of the toothed cetaceans. Called *Physeter catodon* by scientists, the sperm is famous because it was once abundant in most of the world's seas and was thus a favorite prize of Yankee whalers for a century and a half; as such, it became the protagonist of Herman Melville's classic, *Moby Dick* (see pages 34–39). Because of its size (up to 60 feet), toothed lower jaw and powerful tail, the sperm was a challenging catch for the 18th- and 19th-century whalers who had to seek out the great creature, pursue it in their small boats and harpoon it at close range and considerable risk. But because the sperm's commercial value was so great, whalers judged the risks worth taking. And in the 20th century, modern whaling techniques reduced the dangers while profits remained substantial. As a result—though sperms are now protected by international treaty and appear to be increasing in numbers—they are still high on the list of rare and endangered animals.

The sperm whale takes its English name from a mistaken identification of an oily, waxlike substance that is found in the big cetacean's elongated, squared-off head, which represents a third of its entire body. This substance hardens into a wax when exposed to the air. Early whalers believed it to be a great reserve of semen and named it spermaceti. Commercial whalers have long placed a high premium on spermaceti, as it was found to be an extraordinarily high-grade wax, valuable in the manufacture of luxury candles, face creams and ointments.

The sperm whale's huge appetite for squid and cuttlefish generates a by-product that is even more valuable commercially than spermaceti. This substance is ambergris, a secretion that seems to be produced as a way of protecting the whale's massive alimentary canal from the rock-hard squid beak or the cuttlefish's cuttlebone, a kind of internal shell. When it is exposed to air, ambergris solidifies into a waxlike substance that is an excellent fixative for the delicate scents in luxury perfumes. Although synthetic fixatives have been developed, ambergris is still very much in demand: A 920-pound lump, washed up on an Australian beach in 1953, sold for $120,000.

Melville was truly borrowing from legend when he created Moby Dick as a white whale. Although albinos do occur among the cetaceans, *P. catodon* is normally mottled gray. Among the Odontoceti there is, however, one truly white whale, also known as the beluga, derived from the Russian word for "white." Of modest size, reaching a maximum of 18 feet, the beluga is unique among all the cetaceans for its color. It is a circumpolar species, living out its 20 or so years of life in high Arctic and adjacent waters. Belugas travel in small family groups, feeding on crabs, cuttlefish and bottom-dwelling fish such as flounder and halibut. They occasionally swim up Arctic rivers.

A close cousin of the beluga is the narwhal, a 15-foot creature right out of medieval mythology: a maritime unicorn with the sleek, streamlined body of a true whale, topped off with an astonishing, spearlike tooth. The narwhal has only two teeth, which grow horizontally forward from the upper jaw. For reasons that are not well understood, the left tooth of the adult male keeps growing, taking on a spiral, tapering shape and extending as much as nine feet. Perhaps the male narwhal's tusk is pure adornment. It is not used for combat. Whatever its purpose, the narwhal's tusk has contributed to its near extinction, for whalers hunted this curious-looking animal not only for the oil from its blubber but also for the ivory. Many a narwhal tusk, touted as the horn of the mythical unicorn, has been sold for more than its weight in gold to superstitious and affluent men who believed it to possess magical powers for the restoration of health and sexual vigor. In the Middle Ages an Elector of Saxony paid 100,000 talers (one taler was worth a week's wages) for a single tusk, and the Prussian Kaiser, Karl V, paid off a national debt with two.

Sperm whale

"There She Blows!"

Some whales travel in sociable herds, or pods; others are solitary. Only the big sperm whales gather in harems, with half a dozen or more females living around a single bull. In fierce contests for the harems, old bulls are sometimes driven off by younger, stronger males and forced into involuntary bachelorhood. Such deposed loners often become irritable and aggressive (one of these rogue whales was the prototype of Moby Dick).

In the surfacing seraglio below, the sperm whale at left, top, is spouting—exhaling stale, warm air that condenses into vapor upon contact with the cold surface air. One of the main differences between the two suborders of cetaceans is that the toothed whales have just one blowhole, while all baleens have two. Each species has a distinctive way of spouting, which experienced whalers can recognize and readily identify. In the case of the sperm whale, the spout is a forward gush of spray which is emitted at a 45-degree angle that clearly indentifies the species and, in the old whaling days, was the signal for the hunting cry "There she blows!"

Opening its blowhole as it nears the surface, a beluga whale (above) releases a cascade of bubbles that, when it reaches the chilly air, explodes into a geyser of vapor. Belugas inhabit the frigid coastal waters of the Arctic Ocean, sometimes venturing south as far as the North and Baltic seas. In 1966 a lone beluga swam nearly 250 miles up the Rhine and a month later swam back to sea again.

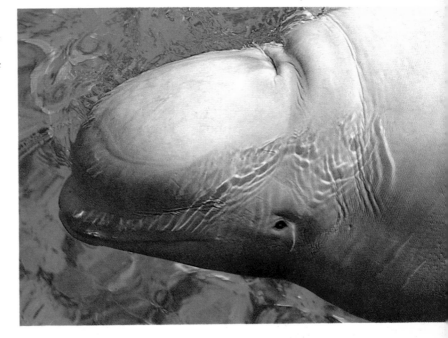

A beluga closes its blowhole to a waterproof slit in the photograph at right. Because they inhale relatively small amounts of air and have a supply of oxygen from specially adapted blood vessels, whales are in no danger of getting the "bends," the effect of nitrogen bubbles that get into the blood of deep-diving humans and can cause death if surfacing is too rapid.

The origin of the pilot whale's name is not clear, though some experts attribute it to the mindless pursuit an entire pod of pilot whales will give to a single runaway member. Others believe the name derives from the whales' habit of following schools of herring, "piloting" fishermen to good fishing grounds. Curiously, pilot whales, like the one at left, frequently beach themselves, often en masse. Puzzled cetologists now suspect that the cause is ear parasites, which foil echolocation.

Maritime Unicorns, Fishermen's Friend

With its eight- or nine-foot lancelike tusk, the narwhal (below and in the filmstrip at right) is the most bizarre member of the whale family. The tusk, which occurs in the male only, is an outgrowth of one of the two teeth in the narwhal's upper jaw. Almost invariably it is the left tooth that grows, though on rare occasions the right one also blooms, giving the creature an even odder appearance.

During the superstitious Middle Ages a narwhal tusk, passed off as the magical ivory of a unicorn, was worth more than its weight in gold, and the animal was hunted relentlessly. Later, the narwhal was killed incidentally by Arctic whalers in search of bowhead whales. Since the demise of bowhead whaling, the narwhal has recovered and survives largely undisturbed, for the expense of Arctic whaling is too great in comparison with the insignificant return of the relatively small whale, which grows to a length, excluding tusks, of around 15 feet. Eskimos, who kill the narwhal for its nutritious skin, are about its only remaining predators.

The pilot whale (opposite, above), a somewhat larger member of the toothed tribe, has not been so fortunate. It is still slaughtered for dog food and oil, unprotected by the international agreements that govern the harvesting of the great whales. Usually found in large groups, pilot whales have an odd compulsion to follow maverick members of their pod. Whalers exploit this quirk by harpooning one or two pilots, herding them into shallow water and waiting for the rest of the pod to follow to a mass slaughter.

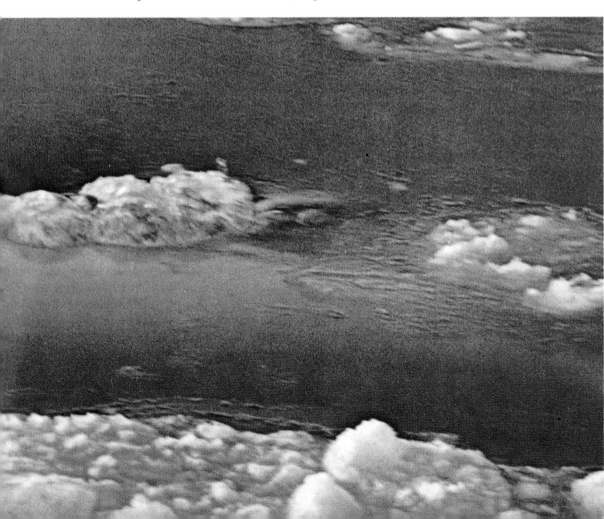

Dolphins and Porpoises

Because most people think of whales as ponderous giants, few are aware that the playful, acrobatic porpoises and their cousins the dolphins are also cetaceans—members of the suborder of toothed whales. Dolphins, in fact, are the most numerous of the cetaceans. Like their larger kin (and like porpoises), they breathe through a single blowhole set high in the head.

Porpoises and dolphins, which are among the world's most sociable animals, belong to the superfamily Delphinoidea. The name is associated with the ancient Greek legend, according to which the god Apollo rose from the sea in the shape of a dolphin and led settlers to Delphi, the place that became the seat of the famed Delphic oracle and a place where Apollo was especially venerated.

The word "porpoise" comes from a contraction of the Latin *porcopiscis*, meaning "pig-fish," and apparently refers to the relative stockiness of the creature the Greeks called *phokaina* and of which Aristotle correctly wrote: "It resembles a small dolphin . . . though it differs from the dolphin by being smaller in size and broader across the back." Modern naturalists point out that the most obvious difference between the dolphin and the porpoise is that the dolphin has a snout or beak, while the porpoise has a rounded-off head. The two names, however, are often used interchangeably.

The common porpoise is the snub-nosed creature familiar to boaters and beachcombers on both sides of the Atlantic and is one of the most highly developed members of the delphinid family, probably inferior in intelligence and learning ability only to the bottle-nosed dolphin and the killer and pilot whales. About six feet long and weighing an average of 100 pounds, *Phocaena phocaena* has a dark-gray body with white markings, small breast flukes and a triangular dorsal fin. It is equally abundant along the Atlantic and Pacific coasts of North America. Dall's porpoise, a handsome, chunky creature with a large white patch on its belly, is also a creature of the northern hemisphere, found on both sides of the North Pacific.

The dolphins are divided into two families and comprise approximately 37 species. The largest of all the dolphins is the killer whale, also known throughout its range as the orca. It owes its fearsome reputation to the fact that it is the only cetacean that feeds on warm-blooded animals, including its giant cousins, the great whales.

Although they are found in all the seas of the world, orcas are most abundant in the frigid waters of the Arctic and Antarctic. They are powerful, extremely agile and the fastest of the cetaceans, reaching speeds of around 30 miles per hour. They are equipped with strong jaws that carry upper and lower rows of large, sharp, conical teeth. Although they eat more fish than warm-blooded flesh, they seem most to enjoy the latter. They feed on seals, sea lions, young walruses, penguins and other sea birds as well as on their delphinid cousins.

Male orcas grow to a length of 30 feet, with six-foot dorsal fins. Females are somewhat smaller. Scientists have had little chance to study the orca's reproductive habits, but it is believed that the gestation period lasts from 13 to 16 months and that newborn orcas may measure eight feet in length.

The two best-known delphinids are the bottle-nosed dolphin (*Tursiops truncatus*) and the common dolphin (*Delphinus delphis*). Bottle-nosed dolphins are particularly numerous on the east coast of the United States and in the Mediterranean, Baltic and Caspian seas, and a subspecies, *Tursiops aduncus*, is found throughout the warm and temperate waters of the Pacific. The common dolphin is found, often in great numbers, in all the warm and temperate seas of the world.

The bottle-nosed dolphin measures between six and 10 feet and is usually gray-black on top, shading toward white on the underside. Probably the dolphin of ancient legend, it is the species most widely used in scientific experiments in the captive state (see pages 110–113).

The smaller common dolphin grows to a length of about eight feet, and its sides are streaked with brown, yellow and white. It has a dark mark running around the eye and tapering to a point at the beak, giving it a pleasant aspect. This is the dolphin frequently noticed convoying ships, jumping completely out of the sea and moving almost erect on its tail flippers while searching the horizon. Finding a ship, the dolphins encircle it, some leading at the bow, some on the sides, all leaping alternately in graceful arching flights of several yards before plunging back into the water. They repeat their nautical capers for hours and hundreds of miles, seemingly without tiring.

Spinner dolphins

Delphinid Duo

Next to the common dolphin, the bottle-nosed dolphin, the comical creature with the smug smile and the distinctive beak seen below, is the best-known and most popular member of the delphinid family. It is most often seen as a performer in aquariums or, under such Disneyesque names as Flipper or Flippy, as the star of film and television shows. A playful, bright and gregarious animal, the bottle-nose has been known to rush to the aid of another disabled dolphin, buoying it up so that it can breathe or nudging it to shallow water. And there are countless stories, including a few that have been authenticated, about bottle-nosed dolphins helping drowning or injured humans.

Native to all the world's oceans, bottlenoses were the principal test animals scientists used to determine the re- markably high intelligence of cetaceans. In the Soviet Union they are a protected species, specifically because their brains are so similar to man's.

Another delphinid without the prominent beak of the dolphin is the harbor porpoise (painting, opposite), which for years was a rare and much prized delicacy among Europeans. Its rarity was more a function of elusiveness than scarcity, though laws were passed in Normandy as early as 1098 regulating the size and number of the annual harbor porpoise harvest. The animal is a fish-eater, preferring herring, whiting and sole, and it frequently swims dozens of miles up rivers pursuing prey. One harbor porpoise was observed more than 200 miles from the sea in the Netherlands' Maas River.

THE LIVING SEA
by Jacques-Yves Cousteau

Many people have seen dolphins frolicking in the ocean or at aquarium shows, but few have had the opportunity of witnessing an entire seascape filled with the cavorting creatures. Jacques-Yves Cousteau, the world-famous undersea explorer, author and television entrepreneur, and the crew of his yacht, Calypso, *had just such a rare experience while cruising in the Indian Ocean off the coast of Arabia. As Cousteau describes the scene in the following excerpt from his book* The Living Sea, *the waters exploded with leaping, racing and diving dolphins—a dazzling 20,000 strong.*

Simone and I turned out, feeling underfoot the first long, indolent swells of the Indian Ocean. We went to the port rail, yawning and stretching, and looked at the burnt, bare-boned Hadramaut Coast of Arabia. *Calypso* was on an easting in the Sea of Oman.

The phone rang in my quarters. In urgent tones, unusual for him, Saôut said, "Can you come to the bridge?" I found him thumbing through our largest-scale charts. "There is no reef here," the skipper announced.

"What reef?" I demanded.

"A tremendous reef—thick, white water dead ahead," he replied.

I bounded to the wheelhouse and took up my binoculars. Some miles ahead, there was a barrier of foam across the horizon. "There can't be a reef here in the ship lane," I said.

"Then what is it?" Saôut asked.

I replied, "Stay on course. We'll find out."

The reef seemed to sway. A half-mile from it we saw that the splashing breakers were composed of leaping dolphins, the most formidable host that either Saôut or I had seen in a quarter of a century at sea. He rang the bridgehouse bell to rouse out everyone to see them. The dolphin army wheeled and charged toward us in a storm comber that erupted twisting black bodies into the air. A nation of dolphins had gone mad before our eyes.

Dolphins, of course, are air-breathing mammals, and we were familiar with their light, measured prancing into the air to breathe. But these were shooting vertically high out of the water, bending and contorting in the leap. It was a mass high-jump contest, a bridal feast, or a frenzied victory celebration after some unknown war in the deep. We jostled each other in the companionways, running for cameras and scrambling for the high bridge and the underwater observatory.

For the rest of the day *Calypso* was steered by dolphins,

obeying the whims of the flying phalanx spreading before us to either rim of the ocean. I took a rough sighting on their jumps. The tails were clearing twelve to fifteen feet. As they fell, they twisted into awkward postures, as if vying to smack the water in the most ungraceful way. I tried to estimate how many there were. At a given minute, there were about a thousand out of the water on jumps that averaged three seconds. For one in the air, there must have been nineteen in the water. Perhaps twenty thousand dolphins formed the living reef.

The massive crescent of foam and flying bodies, glistening in the sun, moved along the Hadramaut Coast with no apparent destination, given up to some titanic collective joy. We shouted like children and bet on leaps. Two dozen amateur cameramen tried to anticipate and film the record high jumps of the dolphin Olympic games.

From the underwater chamber the sight was apocalyptic. The radius of transparency was about a hundred feet, a sphere packed with streaming bodies, effortlessly maintaining the pace of *Calypso*. Some dolphins hung close to the windows of the observatory, eying the men inside. The escort was crisscrossed by dolphins charging across the bow with flickering speed. Through this fleeting, cross-hatching pack there was also an astounding vertical movement. Dolphins sped straight up from the deep, threw themselves into a sort of secondary rocket-booster stage in front of the windows, and shot through the glittering ceiling. They belly-flopped back into the water, collected themselves, and sounded, printing a white trail of exhalations in the blue. Down there on their vapory launching pads, these living missiles began another take-off past the windows into the sun.

We were so enthralled by the three-dimensional carnival that we did not hear imploring yells from the top of the entry tube: "Hey, you people have been down there long enough! Give somebody else a chance." At dusk the pack left *Calypso*, and she got back into the business of being a ship instead of a plaything for dolphins. We waited for the stars to come out to tell us where they had led us.

On many occasions in the Atlantic and Indian oceans we have come upon hundreds of porpoises or dolphins, but no herd as large or as tirelessly berserk as the legion of the Hadramaut. In all other encounters they were moving in orderly formation, apparently agreed on where they were going. They would detour from the route march to satisfy their invariable curiosity about *Calypso*, then take up course again. It was quite rare to see one perform a high jump. Nor did we understand the goals of these migrations, for several times we saw two disciplined packs passing each other in opposite directions with no apparent fraternization.

Dolphins like to play in the late afternoon and occasionally they remained with us some hours after dark. When night found them around *Calypso*, I was selfish about the underwater chamber. Then their show was written in sparkling sequins of plankton. As the dolphins arched their backs, a ghost animal formed in the water and streamed back to the window in a glowing contrail. This black-and-jade farandole had a bewitching visual rhythm and a lively orchestral accompaniment. The resonant chamber amplified their twittering patter of song.

Dolphins *may* be able to speak. However, if it was conversation that we heard on sonar, hydrophones, and in submerged chambers, it was not articulated like human speech. The dolphin does not have a throat, tongue, and lip equipment to pronounce words, but makes shrill, modulated sounds. There are at least two places in the world where men still use a modulated type of language. In the Pyrenées and the Canary Islands there is a whistling speech that carries much further than glottal expression. Canary Island shepherds on crags three miles apart converse in a whistling language that has a considerable vocabulary. This *may* be the dolphin's technique as well.

In a school the usual flow of high-pitched dolphin chirps was interpolated with distinctly different grunts and croaks in low register that did not seem to belong to the "language." The bass tones may have been echo-ranging impulses, as distinguished from gossip.

51

Considering their complicated social behavior and the growing suspicion that they might talk, some specialists do not rule out the possibility that the dolphins, porpoises, and toothed whales have a folklore, an oral preceptorial and storytelling tradition passed from generation to generation in the deeps of time. *If* they have a language and we can someday decipher it, man may learn something of the history of the sea. *Calypso* often induced such indefensible dreams of the space below.

Sometimes on nights of dead calm I stood on the foredeck and spotted ahead, a hundred feet or so, a frightened splash and an opalescent trail coming toward me. I looked down at a dancing wraith, a dolphin or porpoise—followed by more mammals streaking to the ship. *Calypso* had awakened a tribe sleeping on the surface. Like many wild animals, dolphins probably sleep with one eye open in the direction of predators—in this case sharks—and close the other on the secure side, the air. By day the lightning dolphin need fear no rival, but in bed it is vulnerable and maintains a highly tensed alarm system. I imagine sea mammals have many restless nights.

The young dolphin stays with its mother until grown about half her size, then it leaves and joins a gang of other adolescents. These youthful packs are full of vigor, eager to devastate the sea. *Calypso* often chased them but was never able to get among them. They are not interested in playing with ships.

In the Amirantes we had a rare glimpse of the dolphin's private life. I was taking a diving party by launch along the north cape of Daros Island when two dozen adults swam around the corner and stopped to fool around the boat. We harnessed up and dropped in with them. The dolphins were not at all disturbed. Indeed, they seemed to welcome an opportunity to show off some stunts. Several pairs marched away like duelists, turned, and drove toward each other. At the last moment, they avoided bashing heads. The rest lolled around, resting flippers on a friend's back, lazing in the shallows, or turning up their bellies to scratch their backs on the rocks. At Daros, the tireless racers of the open sea seemed to be on vacation.

The Cradle of the Deep

After a gestation period of almost a year, a bottle-nosed dolphin cow (above) gives birth to a calf. Unlike most mammals, cetaceans are usually born tail first. The first moments after birth are crucial for the newborn dolphin, which, because it has no air in its lungs, tends to sink and is thus in danger of suffocating. Therefore, once her calf is born, the cow concentrates her efforts on nudging it to the surface of the water as quickly as possible for its first lungful of air. The cow appears to be aided in the delivery and early care of her calf by other cows from the pod. Such "aunts" seem to display an instinctive desire to protect the cow during this period of extreme vulnerability.

The newborn calf begins to suckle soon after birth and continues to do so about once every half hour, 24 hours a day for its first few weeks of life. Nursing dolphins stay close to their mothers' sides and are left alone on the water's surface for only the few moments it takes the cow to find food herself. By the time the calf is six months old, feedings have dropped to about seven a day. Calves continue to nurse until they are from 12 to 20 months old, by which time they have been gradually introduced to the squids and fish that will make up their entire diet.

54

As its mother swims slowly around their tank (left), a young bottle-nosed dolphin nurses on milk that has been described as tasting like a mixture of "fish, liver, milk of magnesia and oil." Underwater, the mother releases the milk into the calf's funnellike lips and mouth. This is a most efficient method of feeding, insuring the calf of maximum nourishment in a minimum amount of time, since a calf is able to stay submerged for only 30 seconds. A bottle-nosed cow (below) uses this limitation to discipline her errant calf. By holding it down near the bottom of the tank with her mouth, she prevents the calf from surfacing for air just long enough to make her displeasure known.

Killers: True and False

One of the most intelligent of all animals, the killer whale (below and on the cover) also has the reputation of being one of the most savage. It is the only cetacean with a taste for warm blood and readily preys on sea lions, seals and even other cetaceans. A pod of killers will unhestitatingly take on the largest baleen whale, chopping at its head and mouth until it is exhausted and then feasting on the most tender parts until satisfied, leaving the rest of the dying giant to other predators.

Paradoxically, killer whales are surprisingly docile in their relations with man, and there is no authenticated report of them ever having killed or injured a human, although they are quite capable of doing so. In captivity they are friendly and affectionate, and, because of their keen intelligence and learning ability, they are invariably one of the star performers in aquariums.

The closely related, equally intelligent false killer whale (opposite) got its name solely because of its resemblance to the authentic killer. It feeds on cuttlefish and squids and inhabits deep-water ranges in all the oceans.

Two killer whales swim into surprisingly shallow water off a desolate Patagonian shore in pursuit of a herd of sea lions. The sea lions, aware that they are secure on the beach, seem to be taunting the killers, with some of the more daring youngsters even venturing to the water's edge just out of reach of their enemies.

58

Unlike the sea lions on the opposite page, this hapless Weddell seal is doomed—trapped on an Antarctic ice floe by three killer whales. To catch their prey, the killers will lunge partly up on the ice, break up the floe by ramming it with their heads or will fling showers of icy water at the seal with their fins. In such a situation the seal is likely to panic and slide off into the water to certain death.

SCOTT'S LAST EXPEDITION *by Robert Falcon Scott*

In 1911 two veteran polar explorers, Roald Amundsen of Norway and Robert Falcon Scott, a British naval officer, captured the attention of the world with their dramatic race to be the first to reach the South Pole. Amundsen won the race, reaching the pole one month before Scott. Scott's historic journey ended in tragedy, for he and his companions perished in a blizzard. The diary that Scott had kept throughout the expedition was recovered, and it is from this remarkable work, Scott's Last Expedition, *that the following account of an extraordinary encounter with killer whales is excerpted.*

"1911, Thursday, January 5—All hands were up at 5:00 this morning and at work at 6:00. Words cannot express the splendid way in which everyone works and gradually the work gets organized. I was a little late on the scene this morning, and thereby witnessed a most extraordinary scene. Some 6 or 7 killer whales, old and young, were skirting the fast floe edge ahead of the ship; they seemed excited and dived rapidly, almost touching the floe. As we watched, they suddenly appeared astern, raising their snouts out of water. I had heard weird stories of these beasts, but had never associated serious danger with them. Close to the water's edge lay the wire stern rope of the ship, and our two Esquimaux dogs were tethered to this. I did not think of connecting the movements of the whales with this fact, and seeing them so close I shouted to Ponting, who was standing abreast of the ship. He seized his camera and ran towards the floe edge to get a close picture of the beasts, which had momentarily disappeared. The next moment the whole floe under him and the dogs heaved up and split into fragments. One could hear the 'booming' noise as the whales rose under the ice and struck it with their backs [more probably their rostral beaks, J.C.L]. Whale after whale rose under the ice, setting it rocking fiercely; luckily Ponting kept his feet and was able to fly to security. By an extraordinary chance also, the splits had been made around and between the dogs, so that neither of them fell into the water. Thus it was clear that the whales

shared our astonishment, for one after another their huge hideous heads shot vertically into the air through the cracks which they had made. As they reared them to a height of 6 or 8 feet it was possible to see their tawny head markings, their small glistening eyes, and their terrible array of teeth—by far the largest and most terrifying in the world. There cannot be a doubt that they looked up to see what had happened to Ponting and the dogs.

"The latter were horribly frightened and strained to

their chains, whining; the head of one killer must certainly have been within 5 feet of one of the dogs.

"After this, whether they thought the game insignificant, or whether they missed Ponting is uncertain, but the terrifying creatures passed on to other hunting grounds, and we were able to rescue the dogs, and what was even more important, our petrol—5 or 6 tons of which was waiting on a piece of ice which was not split away from the main mass.

"Of course, we have known well that killer whales continually skirt the edge of floes and that they would undoubtedly snap up anyone who was unfortunate enough to fall into the water; but the fact that they could display such deliberate cunning, that they were able to break ice of such thickness (at least 2½ feet), and that they could act in unison, were a revelation to us. It is clear that they are endowed with singular intelligence, and in the future we shall treat that intelligence with every respect."

Manatees and Dugongs

"I saw three mermaids," Christopher Columbus wrote matter-of-factly in his log, "but they were not as beautiful as they are painted."

Columbus had no doubt that the creatures he saw in the Caribbean waters were indeed mermaids. Actually they were manatees. It is difficult to understand how anyone ever mistook these blubbery gray animals with their wrinkled skin and whiskery faces for the alluring sea maidens of romantic legend. Yet the notion persisted for 2,500 years before Columbus and lingers on today. So strongly has the myth become entrenched in sea lore and literature that the order that includes manatees and their Old World cousins, dugongs, is called Sirenia.

Homer probably started the mermaid legend with his descriptions of sweet-voiced sirens who beset Ulysses and his men with temptation, and Pliny the Elder, a reputable naturalist in his day (23 to 79 A.D.), gave it credence, warning those who were skeptical of mermaids: "It is no fabulous tale that is told about them; for look how painters draw them—so they are indeed, only their body is rough and scaled all over, even in those parts where they resemble a woman."

The sirenians fit between whales and seals in the evolutionary aquacade of mammals that have adapted to life in the water. They retain such characteristics of land animals as lungs and limbs that evolved into flippers but are completely helpless on land, not even able to crawl about as seals and otters do. On the other hand, they are able, unlike whales, to maneuver out of shallows to the safety of deep water. Mating and birth take place under water, and the male manatee remains with his mate even after the breeding season. The female is an attentive mother, suckling her single pup and allowing it to ride on her back when it is tired. Strict vegetarians, manatees consume great quantities of shallow-water grasses: A single manatee will eat at least 60 pounds of water plants in a day. Because of their voracious appetites they are of some service to mankind, keeping coastal waterways free and unclogged by such growth as water hyacinth.

The chief differences between manatees and dugongs are in habitat and anatomical details. The manatee inhabits both the sea and inland rivers and lakes. The dugong, however, is strictly a saltwater mammal, living in coastal areas where it can feed on shallow-water grasses. The dugong's head is larger and its flippers shorter than the manatee's. The dugong's tail is notched, unlike the rounded one of the manatee.

There is only a single species of dugong, large numbers of which were once found in coastal areas throughout the Indian Ocean, in the Red Sea and the South China Sea. But, hunted extensively for its savory flesh and the oil from its blubber, it is now found only in isolated areas of its old habitat and in greatly reduced numbers.

Manatees have developed three species: the northern manatee, with a range from the southeastern United States to northern South America; the Brazilian, a freshwater species of the Amazon and Orinoco rivers; and the African, a creature of the coast, rivers and lakes of West Africa. They too have been extensively hunted, though the northern manatee is now protected in Florida.

Neither the manatee nor the dugong frequent Arctic waters. The only sirenian that ever did—the Northern, or Steller, sea cow—is extinct. It was a huge animal, some 25 feet in length. The story of its discovery and extermination is one of the most tragic in the long and bloody history of man's treatment of other animals. Georg Wilhelm Steller (see pages 68–69), the physician and naturalist of Captain Vitus Bering's Russian expedition to the northern Pacific in 1741–42, discovered the enormous, peaceful mammal off the coast of one of the Commander Islands when his ship was wrecked. Steller made voluminous notes on its physical and behavioral characteristics and correctly identified it as a huge, hitherto unknown member of the sirenian order. But because Steller and his companions were desperate for food, they killed and consumed the meat of several of the bovine creatures. With their ship repaired, they returned to Russia carrying the valuable furs of several hundred sea otters and Arctic foxes they had also killed for food. When word got around that there was a fortune in furs ready for the taking in the Commanders, hunters by the hundreds descended on the area and found that the meat of the Steller sea cow was tasty and easily come by. They quickly wiped out this largest of the sirenians. Twenty-seven years after it was discovered, Steller sea cow was no more. It has been listed as extinct for more than 200 years, and the only records of this gentle giant are a few bits of skin and bone in museums and the descriptions contained in the journals of Steller—possibly the only naturalist ever simultaneously to discover a species and to become the unwitting instrument of its extinction.

62

Vegetarian Mermaid

The only herbivores among the marine mammals, sirenians consume prodigious amounts of aquatic plants. An adult manatee, weighing as much as 1,500 pounds, needs an abundance of vegetation to maintain its blubbery weight and can easily eat as much as 60 pounds a day. Native manatees, for example, have been introduced on the sugarcane plantations of Guyana to keep weed-choked canals cleared. When it eats, a manatee uses its flippers in a very human way to guide the water plants to its mouth, which may account for its association with the mermaid myth.

By nature, sirenians are among the gentlest of animals. They become quite tame and trusting in captivity and will readily come to the surface to take vegetable offerings from their keepers' hands. Only in those areas of the world, such as some parts of India, where they have been hunted to near extinction for their flesh and oils have they become shy and elusive.

In their adaptation to aquatic life, manatees have lost their hind legs altogether and have grown tails, shaped like large palmetto fans (right), that propel them through the water. Dugongs, their Old World cousins, have more fishlike, squared-off rudders. The sirenians' forepaws have become flippers (above), which they employ to shovel food into their mouths or to cradle nursing babies.

Endangered Dugongs

Another sea mammal to join the ever-growing list of animals that have suffered, perhaps irreversibly, at the hands of man is the dugong (opposite). Hunted for its meat, which is considered a delicacy in places such as Madagascar, the dugong is also pursued for its blubber and the fine oil it produces. Once abundant in the warm waters of the Indian Ocean and the western Pacific, this benign and bulky creature (adults grow to about 10 feet in length and weigh over 600 pounds) seems, in many parts of its range, to be following in the footsteps of its now extinct relative, the Steller sea cow.

The dugong leads a slow-paced, peaceful life. It is thought that the animal rests in deep water during the day, moving to shallower, inland water at night to feed on algae and aquatic grasses. The dugong rips the plants from the sea bottom, swishing them clean with a shake of its head. When the vegetation is sand-free, the dugong stuffs it into its mouth with its flippers. (Elephants, which are thought to be distantly related to dugongs, clean their food in a similar fashion.) Dugongs have been seen storing piles of sea grass along shorelines, eating them only after the sand contained in them has had time to settle. Although a dugong is capable of remaining underwater for up to 10 minutes at a time, an undisturbed animal will usually stop feeding every minute or so to come to the surface for air.

During the 19th century large herds of dugongs were often sighted traveling along the northern coast of Australia. Today, however, dugongs are considered solitary animals. Pairs are occasionally sighted, but family groups of three or more members are exceedingly rare.

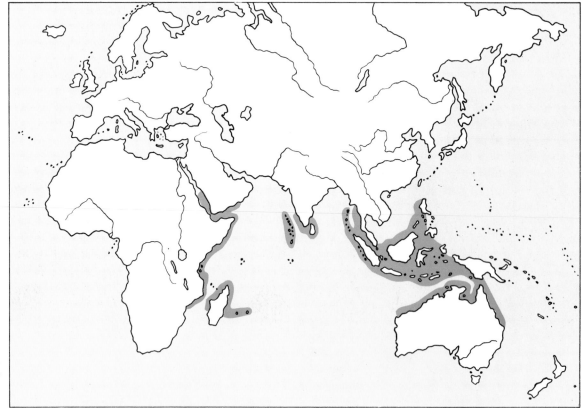

Dugongs are now sparsely scattered through areas where they were once numerous. They inhabit the coastal waters of the entire Indian Ocean from the east coast of Africa to the Red Sea, as well as the waters around Taiwan, the southeastern Philippines and the northern coast of Australia, shown in dark blue. But due to extensive hunting of the species throughout its range, the dugong is now considered an endangered species.

BEASTS OF THE SEA

by Georg Wilhelm Steller

Georg Wilhelm Steller, a German naturalist, joined Vitus Bering's expedition to the northern Pacific in 1741. Their ship was wrecked, and the explorers spent eight miserable months on a bleak island. While he was marooned, Steller made studies of the local animals, as described on page 62. One was later named Steller sea cow in the naturalist's honor but soon became extinct. Steller's description, from his Beasts of the Sea, *follows.*

Every day for ten months during our ill-fated adventure [he says] I had a chance to watch from the door of my hut the behavior and habits of these creatures and I will therefore briefly relate what I actually observed.

These animals love shallow and sandy places along the seashore, but they spend their time more particularly about the mouths of the gullies and brooks, the rushing fresh water of which always attracts them in herds. They keep the half-grown and young in front of them when pasturing, and are very careful to guard them in the rear and on the sides when traveling, always keeping them in the middle of the herd. With the rising tide they come in so close to the shore that not only did I on many occasions prod them with a pole or a spear, but sometimes even stroked their back with my hand. If badly hurt they did nothing more than move farther away from shore, but after a while they forgot their injury and came back. Usually entire families keep together, the male with the female, one grown offspring and a little, tender one. To me they appear to be monogamous. They bring forth their young at all seasons, generally however in autumn, judging from the many new-born seen at that time; from the fact that I observed them to mate preferably in the early spring, I conclude that the fetus remains in the uterus more than a year. That they bear not more than one calf I conclude from the shortness of the uterine cornua and the dual number of mammae, nor have I ever seen more than one calf about each cow.

These gluttonous animals eat incessantly, and because of their enormous voracity keep their heads always under water with but slight concern for their life and security, so that one may pass in the very midst of them in a boat even unarmed and safely single out from the herd the one he wishes to hook. All they do while feeding is to lift the nostrils every four or five minutes out of the water, blowing out air and a little water with a noise like that of a horse snorting. While browsing they move slowly forward, one foot after the other, and in this manner half swim, half walk like cattle or sheep grazing. Half the body is always out of the water. Gulls are in the habit of sitting on the backs of the feeding animals feasting on the vermin infesting the skin, as crows are wont to do on the lice of hogs and sheep. They do not eat all kinds of seaweeds promiscuously, but select (1) the wrinkled kind with leaves like Savoy cabbage and latticed (crispum Brassicae Sabaudicae folio cancellatum); (2) the weed looking like a club (fucum clavae facie [Nereocystes]); (3) the weed like an old Roman lash (fucum scuticae antiquae Romanae facie); (4) the very long weed with the edges of the leaves wavy along the midrib (fucum longissimum limbis in nervum undulatis [Laminaria]). Where they have been staying even for a single day there may be seen immense heaps of roots and stems. Some of them when their bellies are full, go to sleep lying on their backs, first moving some distance away from shore so as not to be left on dry land by the outgoing tide. In winter they often become smothered by the ice floating along the shore and are cast up on the beach dead, which also happens if they get crushed against the rocks by the waves breaking fiercely among the cliffs. In winter these animals become so emaciated that not only the ridge of the backbone but every rib shows.

In the spring they mate like human beings, particularly towards evening when the sea is calm. Before they come together many amorous preludes take place. The female, constantly followed by the male, swims leisurely to and fro eluding him with many gyrations and meanderings, until, impatient of further delay, she turns on her back as if exhausted and coerced, whereupon the male, rushing violently upon her, pays the tribute of his passion, and both give themselves over in mutual embrace.

Their capture was effected by a large iron hook, the point of which somewhat resembled the fluke of an anchor, the other end being fastened by means of an iron ring to a very long and stout rope, held by thirty men on shore. A strong sailor took this hook and with four or five other men stepped into the boat, and one of them taking the rudder, the other three or four rowing, they quietly hurried towards the herd. The harpooner stood in the bow of the boat with the hook in his hand and struck as soon as he was near enough to do so, whereupon the men on shore, grasping the other end of the rope, pulled the desperately resisting animal laboriously towards them. Those in the boat, however, made the animal fast by means of another rope and wore it out with continual blows, until, tired and completely motionless, it was attacked with bayonets, knives and other weapons and pulled up on land. Immense slices were cut from the still living animal, but all it did was shake its tail furiously and make such resistance with its forelimbs that big strips of the cuticle were torn off. In addition it breathed heavily, as if sighing. From the wounds in the back the blood spurted upward like a fountain. As long as the head was under water no blood flowed, but as soon as it raised the head up to breathe the blood gushed forth anew. . . . The old and very large animals were much more easily captured than the calves, because the latter moved about much more vigorously, and were likely to escape, even if the hook remained unbroken, by its tearing through the skin, which happened more than once.

When an animal caught with the hook began to move about somewhat violently, those nearest in the herd began to stir also and feel the urge to bring succor. To this end some of them tried to upset the boat with their backs, while others pressed down the rope and endeavored to break it, or strove to remove the hook from the wound in the back by blows of their tail, in which they actually succeeded several times. It is a most remarkable proof of their conjugal affection that the male, after having tried with all his might, although in vain, to free the female caught by the hook, in spite of the beating we gave him, nevertheless followed her to the shore, and that several times, even after she was dead, he shot unexpectedly up to her like a speeding arrow. Early next morning, when we came to cut up the meat and bring it to the dugout, we found the male again standing by the female, and the same I observed once more on the third day when I went there by myself for the sole purpose of examining the intestines.

The drawing below of the Steller sea cow was done in 1826 and was based on a sketch made by Friedrich Plenisner, a draftsman with the 1741 Bering expedition.

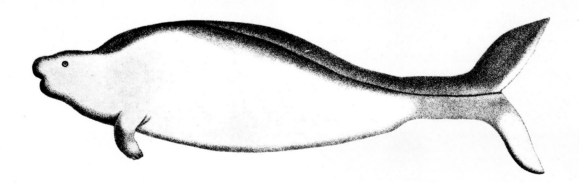

Seals, Sea Lions and Walruses

Pinnipedia, translated "finfooted," is the accurately descriptive name scientists have given to the suborder of marine mammals that includes the seal, the sea lion, the elephant seal and the walrus. The pinnipeds, while more at home in the water than on land, still retain the four limbs that were characteristic of their terrestrial ancestors and can move about on shore with varying degrees of agility. All pinnipeds come ashore to bear their young and to molt. Most mate on shore and some prefer to sleep on land or ice, safe from killer whales and sharks.

Despite 200 years of unremitting slaughter by man, an estimated 25 million pinnipeds still crowd breeding beaches and dive for food in all the seas, the vast majority preferring the colder waters at the northern and southern extremes of the planet. A few species, notably leopard seals, attack fellow warm-blooded animals such as penguins and other seals. All feed on fish and other forms of cold-blooded marine life. The pinnipeds range in size from the little ringed seal, which reaches an adult length of less than five feet, to the giant and occasionally pugnacious southern elephant seal, which may be more than 20 feet long and weigh in excess of four tons.

The suborder includes some 30 species, divided into three major groupings: eared seals (Otariidae), true seals (Phocidae) and walruses (Odobenidae). As their name suggests, the eared seals, which include sea lions and fur seals, have retained visible external ears; true seals and walruses lack such external protuberances and thus are more streamlined for submarine movement. Another difference between the otarids and phocids is in their manner of swimming. The eared seals use their powerful forelimbs in a kind of breast stroke as the main source of swimming power, their rear limbs remaining almost motionless. The earless seals propel themselves through the water with a strong sculling movement of the hind flippers. The walruses combine the two methods, using mainly their forelimbs to move their big bodies.

Pinnipeds are not only fast swimmers, capable of reaching speeds of 15 to 18 miles per hour for short distances; they are also expert divers. Many can remain under water without breathing for extended periods. A Weddell seal, which thrives in cold Antarctic waters, has been clocked at 70 minutes under water and has carried a depth recorder to 1,968 feet below the surface.

During their breeding season most pinnipeds leave the water and return to well-established nuptial beaches. Some are polygamous, with bulls establishing harems each year and lording it over as many as 15 cows, which arrive at the beaches ready to give birth, carrying pups conceived in the previous year's mating. Although a few species mate only once in two years, most mate annually, with bulls returning early to remembered shores to establish their territories and wait for the females to arrive, join a harem and bear their pups. Almost immediately after giving birth, females mate again. The elephant seal bulls are noted for their ferocity in defending their territory and harems. Bulls engage in bloody fights and often seriously wound one another, but fatalities are rare.

The length of time pups are suckled depends on species and habitat. Pinnipeds from the coldest climates have the shortest lactation periods—two to three weeks for many polar seals in comparison to six months for the sea lion of temperate waters.

The best-known member of the pinniped family is the California sea lion, the "trained seal" of circuses and zoos, which displays great intelligence and an eager ability to learn various tricks—from playing volleyball to blowing "God Bless America" on a series of horns. Sleek animals with big, soft brown eyes, sea lions are naturally playful, chasing one another in the water while sounding off with much honking and barking. Before they became popular as circus performers they were hunted for their blubber.

The phocids, or earless seals, include 15 species distributed all over the world, ranging from the tropical monk seals that inhabit the Mediterranean and parts of the Pacific around Hawaii, to the Weddell seal, which spends some of its time beneath the Antarctic ice, using a breathing hole to stay alive.

The walrus is placed in a category by itself. One of the largest of the pinnipeds (only the elephant seal is bigger), it is distinguished by its powerful tusks, beard and a gentle but curious disposition. Unfortunately the walrus also has considerable commercial value. In addition to its hide and its blubber it has two-foot tusks of high-quality ivory. So uncontrolled has been the slaughter of this creature that its survival as a species is in considerable doubt. One of the early hunters' cruelest tricks was to catch a pup and beat it until it cried. Its laments brought every adult walrus in the vicinity rushing to its aid—walruses are devoted parents—and to certain death at the hands of the hunters.

Patagonian sea lion

Sea Lion Society

Because they possess tiny but visible external ears, sea lions and fur seals (see pages 78–79) are called eared seals. Sea lions are gregarious creatures that seek out others of their kind whenever they come ashore, using one another as pillows as they laze in the sun.

Tension builds during the mating season, though, when the breeding beaches become bloody battlegrounds as the massive bulls vie for cows and territory. A harem may include as many as a dozen females presided over by a dominant bull, which may be as much as eight feet long and weigh a ton. The bull guards his harem as fiercely as his territorial boundaries. Copulation takes place soon after the birth of the pups so that most cows are pregnant year round. Once a cow has mated with a bull, she goes into the water to feed, returning to the land intermittently to nurse her pup. By this time the bull's good humor has returned to the point where he may even protect the new offspring.

The sea lion couple at right goes through the elaborate courtship ritual that precedes copulation. In this phase the animals move their heads from side to side as they nuzzle and caress each other's neck, face and lips. The pair then moves apart a few steps, raising their snouts into the air. Both bull and cow tease each other before mating actually occurs, after which the bull moves on to another member of his harem.

When the harem bull (on the right, below) lowered his guard over his territory and let his cows take a quick swim, a challenging bull (left) appeared on the scene. But upon returning to land, the bull quickly succeeded in reestablishing his domain and, with a roar of supremacy, drove the intruder away.

Bringing Up Baby

Because they are exhibited in zoos all over the world, California sea lions have come to epitomize all sea lions. There are three separate subspecies of the animal we know as the California sea lion. One is found along the coast of California; a second occurs on the Galápagos Islands off the coast of Ecuador; and the third, a colony on the verge of extinction with a population estimated at only a few animals, inhabits part of the island of Honshu of Japan. On the Galápagos Islands sea lion pups are born between October and December, while their northern Pacific cousins arrive earlier, in May and June. All sea lion cows are attentive, affectionate mothers, but in the Galápagos group, which has been studied closely in the wild, even the bulls share in the care of the young. When a pup enters the water often a bull watches over it, nudging it back to shore if it swims out beyond its depth. It is more common, however, for the cow to play the protector's role, like the California sea lion female at left, which seems to have a firm grip both on her pup and the situation.

At birth a sea lion, like the week-old Galápagos pup above, weighs about 14 pounds and measures less than three feet in length. The pups nurse until they are six months old and then are gradually weaned to an adult diet of squids and octopuses. At maturity sea lion bulls reach seven feet in length and weigh 600 pounds; the cows are a foot shorter and weigh about 200 pounds.

75

In the Galápagos Islands a tense drama unfolds as a female California sea lion (left) realizes that the pup she has just delivered is stillborn. Other females from the harem look on from the water's edge, while on the surrounding rocks four Galápagos hawks take up a grim vigil.

The bereaved mother nudges her baby as if to stir it into life. As the tide comes in she takes the body in her mouth to move it to higher ground. The placenta lies in the sand at left. In the meantime the hawks draw nearer, intent on a certain meal.

On the rocks, the mother carries her dead pup from place to place, while the hawks move closer. In the photograph at right, the claws of a waiting hawk are visible on the rocks at top, left, just a few feet from the mother sea lion. The head of another anxious female sea lion appears at right.

Bowing to the inevitable, the mother finally drops the little body as a hawk moves in brazenly to a spot just out of her reach. And although the mother sea lion will continue to guard her dead pup for a while, the scavenging hawks will be the final winners in the struggle.

The Fur Seals

The Otariidae, or eared seals, also include the fur seals, which are distinguished from their short-haired sea lion cousins by their valuable thick, woolly undercoats. There are eight species in the southern hemisphere but only one, the northern fur seal (the most abundant species of the family), in the northern hemisphere. The largest single population in the north gathers annually, beginning in May, on the breeding beaches on the Pribilof Islands (left). Bulls arrive on land first and battle one another for choice territories for their harems. Fights erupt again when the cows come ashore. Mating takes place a few days after the young are born, and, once all the cows have copulated, the emaciated bulls, which have not fed for about two months, return to the sea. Females stay with the pups until they are weaned and able to swim. Then the pups venture into the sea to feed, and by winter the beaches are virtually deserted.

The soaked northern fur seal at left is one of an estimated population of over one and a half million animals. The resurgence of these animals, which for years had been relentlessly slaughtered for their fur, is a result of an international treaty that protects the seals and permits the killing of only a specified number of young males each year. Similar conservation techniques have been applied to the South American fur seals, such as the one above, in their island habitats off the Uruguayan, Brazilian and Argentinian coasts.

79

a seafarer's tale

*Two ancient legends—one from Scandinavia,
the other from Ireland—have been woven together by
Victor Scheffer to create this delightful tale.*

In the mythos of the folk who make their living from the sea it is well known that hidden in the dark pools of the eyes of certain seals are spirits that call out to certain men. The Irish among us, and a few Scandinavians who have lived long at the edge of the sea, can hear the message best. These seals, they say, are really fisherfolk who were caught in some act displeasing to the gods and were made to live in hairy skins forever after and to wander at the will of the winds and the tides. Once in a while such a seal will save the life of a drowning sailor and will then be released from its beastly bindings. It will turn into a beautiful maid and will be the sailor's wife, but there will be no offspring from the union, and the old women in the village will know the reason why. Always dark-brown of eye and soft of body these beautiful creatures are, and they lie
awake in bed when the full moon streams
through the window.
And their feet are a bit colder than
the feet of ordinary women.

The crabeater seal (right) is probably the most abundant pinniped, with a population estimated at over 10 million individuals, all living around the coasts of Antarctica. Both males and females measure up to nine feet in length and weigh about 500 pounds. The crabeater's diet is made up primarily of krill, its teeth functioning sieve-fashion, like the baleen of some whales. Weddell seals (below) belong to the same subfamily as the crabeaters and, like them, live in the waters around Antarctica.

The Earless Seals

The word "seal" is used to identify a number of pinnipeds that are not true seals. True seals, or phocids, are distinguished by their lack of external ears. The family's 18 species, some of which are seen on these and the following pages, live in the coastal and oceanic waters of virtually every sea and include the largest and smallest among the pinnipeds—the elephant seal and the ringed seal.

Because true seals' forefeet are smaller than their hind feet and are set far forward on their bodies, phocids are less well equipped for life on land than other pinnipeds. They move across ice floes with a laborious, dragging motion and take advantage of any opportunity to roll or slide to their destination instead of crawling. Most earless seals congregate during the breeding season, but rather than forming a large harem, a male establishes a land-based territory and settles down with one female. The couple remains together for the entire mating season.

An inhabitant of the Arctic Pacific, the ribbon seal (left) is one of the smaller pinnipeds; males (somewhat larger than females) grow to a length of five and one half feet and reach weights of more than 200 pounds. Both sexes display distinctive, light-colored ribbon markings around their necks, hindquarters and encircling each flipper. The pattern is more outstanding in males, since their background color is much darker than females'.

Among the phocids, the bearded seal (right) is surpassed only by the elephant seal in size. Bearded males often reach lengths of 10 to 11 feet and weights of 1,000 pounds. Solitary creatures of the Arctic, the bearded seals are named for their handsome whiskers, which serve as probes to help the seal uproot invertebrates such as clams, shrimps, octopuses and sea cucumbers from the sea floor.

Bellowing her fear and fury at an intruder, a harp seal cow (below) fiercely defends her cowering youngster. Harp seal cows are attentive parents and leave their pups only for short intervals during their first icebound weeks of life. Yet if a cow is feeding in the water when her youngster is attacked, she will not come to its defense but will remain in the safety of the sea. Despite its generic name, Pagophilus, meaning ice-lover, harp seals are most secure in the open waters of their Atlantic and Arctic ocean homes.

Except for certain colonies of California sea lions, the monk seals—such as the Hawaiian monk seal (above)—are the only pinnipeds living in tropical waters. They survive in their warm habitats by seeking out cool rocky caves and sand or mud wallows. The Hawaiian monk seal, which inhabits the waters of the northwestern Hawaiian Islands, was given governmental protection in 1909. But human encroachment on their breeding beaches is threatening the species.

The ringed seal is the smallest of the pinnipeds. The whitish pelage of the pup below is different from the adult coat which is marked with whitish rings. Ringed seals are creatures of the far north and, as such, are able to spend considerable time beneath the Arctic ice by making air holes. One hole is always kept large enough for the animal to pass through, giving it access to the top of the ice floes, where it builds a den at pupping time in spring.

Of all seals, probably the most familiar is the black-spotted harbor seal (above), found along the cooler coasts of the northern hemisphere. Most harbor seals live in salt water; a few inhabit freshwater lakes in Canada and Finland. All harbor seals spend some time on land, where they move with a caterpillarlike inching motion. In the water they are propelled by the alternating strokes of their flippers. Harbor seals are generally solitary feeders, eating almost any form of fish, mollusk or crustacean.

A Nose to Make Noise

The giant among the pinnipeds is the elephant seal. There are two species, the larger of which, the southern elephant seal seen on these pages, often grows to a length of 20 feet and an awesome weight of as much as four tons. The northern species rarely reaches 16 feet and weighs an estimated three tons. The common name of these animals comes not only from their great size but also from the unique proboscis of the adult males of both species.

Paradoxically, the nose of the northern elephant seal is bigger than that of its larger southern cousin. Marked off by two wrinkles on the seal's snout—one just beneath the eyes and the other at the point where the trunk slopes downward—this overdeveloped nose is actually an enlarged, inflatable nasal cavity. The trunk is usually limp and deflated (above). But during the breeding season it is blown up, acting as a resonating chamber, amplifying the seal's roar to impress rival bulls (opposite) with whom he must battle for territory and mates.

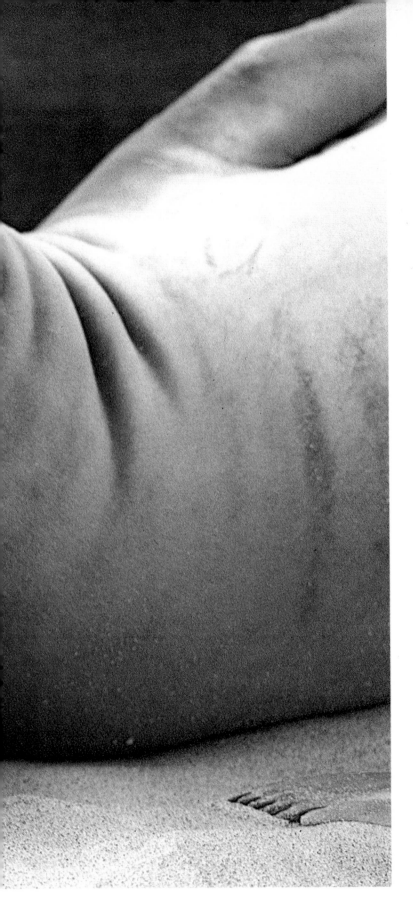

Two cozy young southern elephant seal pups (left) play in the nursery area set up at the back of a rookery on Peninsula Valdes in Argentina. Their frolicsome disposition contrasts sharply with that of the adults, like the two irritable cows above. Breeding cows and bulls fast until the pups have been born, suckled and weaned, a four- to six-week period during which time the level of aggression among all adults remains high. After the calves are weaned, the mature animals return to the sea, where they once again feed on the fish and cephalopods that make up most of their diet.

The Layered Look

Unlike humans, who shed a little of their skin daily, elephant seals molt once a year, a process that may last as long as 40 days. An elephant seal's first molt occurs shortly after its birth—three weeks to one month for the southern species and eight weeks for the northern. The pup's thick black coat is shed first from its back and belly and then from its head, ultimately exposing a silky gray coat that stiffens to the texture of the adult pelage within a year.

Adult elephant seals molt on land during the summer—beginning in May for the northern species and December for the southern. The skin peels off in ragged strips and patches that are strewn along the animals' breeding beaches. Once the molt is completed, the seals return to the sea, where they spend the remainder of the fall and winter feeding.

A young southern elephant seal bull (above) waits out the final stages of his molt. Young and adult seals, like the group at right, often roll in mud wallows, presumably to relieve the itching of their annual ordeal.

The Predatory Leopard Seal

Called the most menacing of all seals, the leopard seal has predatory ways that set it apart from the other phocids. Although it eats krill and fish like the other true seals, the leopard seal's taste also runs to warm-blooded creatures. Lurking patiently around the edges of ice floes in the frigid waters of the Antarctic and sub-Antarctic sea, the 10- to 12-foot-long animals wait for penguins, or other birds and seals which make up much of their diet, to take to the water.

Distinguished by a flat, almost reptilian head and a blunt, rounded snout, the leopard seal is a sure and powerful swimmer. Its main enemy is the fearsome killer whale. However, when the leopard seal comes on land to sleep and, it is believed, to mate and breed, it is rendered less dangerous. Because its flippers are practically useless for locomotion, the seal must move with a strenuous rocking motion, first raising its chest and then its hind parts in order to inch forward over the ice.

The sight of a leopard seal in the water sends a group of Adélie penguins scurrying to the safety of an Antarctic ice floe (left) and refuge from the seal's lethal bite. Not so fortunate, the Adélie at right is quickly taken by a seal, shaken violently and swallowed, feathers and all. After sating its considerable appetite, a leopard seal snoozes on the ice (below) while some Adélies stroll nonchalantly nearby, secure in the knowledge that a land-bound leopard seal is virtually harmless.

With only the top of its large and powerful head breaking the surface of the water, a lone leopard seal patrols the shores of Antarctica for food. Leopard seals are solitary animals. They form pairs or congregate in small groups only during the mating season, which takes place during the Antarctic fall, beginning around February.

94

Toothy Targets

Slaughtered relentlessly by trophy hunters for their fine ivory tusks and by Eskimos and other northern people for their succulent flesh, walruses at one time declined to endangered status. Protective laws of the northern nations where walruses live have largely eliminated the ivory and sport hunters as a menace. However, the local inhabitants, who depend on walrus meat, have been exempted from the prohibition and continue to slaughter the animals.

The distinctive tusks of the walrus (opposite) are used in jousting and as ice axes in climbing onto ice floes. The tusks, which are actually overgrown canine teeth, appear when a young walrus is about five months old (below) and continue to grow for the rest of the animal's life. A single tusk may reach 39½ inches and weigh 11¾ pounds.

The Walrus
Family Circle

In a typical family group, a large, dominant bull presides over a harem of perhaps three cows and half a dozen calves of assorted ages. The calves stay with their mothers until they are four or five years old. They are born with a fine coat of brown fur, which disappears as they grow. The dubious-looking young walrus at left has already lost most of its fur.

The stiff, bristly mustache enables the walrus to locate the mollusks the big animal fancies. Females are devoted mothers, meticulously carrying their babies, nursing them for seven months and occasionally carrying them about on their backs when they swim. Old bulls are not reliable parents: The remains of infant walruses have been found in the stomachs of adult males.

Its impressive tusks are the primary tools of a walrus. They serve as formidable weapons—insurance that the walrus can go its ponderous way with virtually no enemy to fear—except man.

99

Sea Otters

There are 18 species of otters, and all of them live near the water and are good swimmers. But the sea otter has become the most aquatic of them all. It makes infrequent trips ashore—to give birth, to escape from its enemies or to take refuge in a storm—and never ventures more than a few yards from the water's edge. On land it is an ungainly animal, seemingly unable to support its weight on its short legs, but in its watery element the sea otter is a superbly coordinated creature, propelled like a torpedo by its webbed, finlike rear feet. In its most characteristic pose, it floats nonchalantly on its back, with a morsel of food or sometimes a baby otter resting on its chest.

Georg Wilhelm Steller, the German naturalist, made the first scientific study of sea otters during the same Bering expedition to the northern Pacific where he discovered the ill-fated Steller sea cow (see pages 68–69). "A sea otter," he observed, "is by nature a beautiful, pleasant creature with a playful, flattering manner." Though wary, it is generally a friendly creature, tolerating humans who approach its isolated habitats.

The smallest of the marine mammals, measuring four to five feet and weighing up to 100 pounds, the sea otter is protected from the cold by thick and luxuriant fur instead of the blubber that warms other marine mammals. It has retained more of the physiological characteristics of land-dwellers than any of the other mammals that have returned to the sea. It has short, erect ears; five-fingered forepaws, which it uses with considerable dexterity; and well-defined hind legs and finlike feet. Some individual otters seem to prefer to sleep on land, possibly as a safety precaution against their main enemies, the shark and the killer whale. Others get their rest floating on their backs in sheltered waters, with bands of living kelp—which are attached to the ocean bottom—slung across their bodies like safety belts to keep them from drifting out to sea.

With an unsatiable appetite that compels it to consume almost a quarter of its body weight in food each day, a sea otter spends a great deal of time hunting for its meals, which consist of sea urchins, abalone, crabs and other shellfish. In the course of the diving that this search may require, the otter surfaces for air every 30 or 40 seconds (though, when threatened, it can remain submerged for five minutes and plunge to depths of over 300 feet).

In feeding, the sea otter makes remarkable use of tools. When it locates an oyster, for instance, it comes to the surface with a rock in one forepaw, clutching the shellfish to its chest with the other, places the stone and the shellfish on its chest and, floating on its back, breaks the shell against the rock to get at the succulent meat inside. It may also use a rock to pry off bottom-clinging shellfish such as oysters and abalone. This effective employment of a rock as an implement places the sea otter in a highly exclusive and oddly assorted group of tool-users: the chimpanzee, the Galápagos woodpecker finch, the Egyptian vulture and man.

Mating, which may take place at any time of the year, is always accomplished in the water. The sex act may continue as long as 23 minutes, with frequent surfacing for air, and may be repeated several times. The sea otter's gestation period is probably eight to 12 months, and the female generally bears only one pup every other year. Birth takes place in a secluded location on shore, and the mother nurses her pup lying on her back either on land or floating offshore. In time she teaches the baby to swim and, after a year or more of nursing, to forage for solid food. The mother frequently plays with the baby, lifting it up off her chest, then fondling and kissing it. If a pup is threatened, its mother will defend it to the death; and if it is taken from her, she will cry piteously.

Stretched out on its back for a nap, an otter will frequently cover its eyes with a paw to protect them from the glare of sun and water. Otters are quite vocal. Pups cry when they are hungry, females coo affectionately to their mates or their pups, and adults of both sexes scream in severe distress. The otter's call of companionship is a loud squeal that, from a distance, sounds like a whistle.

Because the fur trade has placed such value on its luxuriant pelt, the sea otter very nearly followed its Aleutian neighbor, the Steller sea cow, into extinction. The slaughter of these animals seemed especially cruel, for the otter has been known to nuzzle a hunter about to club it to death or to turn its back on its human killer and cover its eyes with its paws. Once the otter ranged in great numbers from Baja California all along the coast of western North America and westward through the Aleutians and northern Japan. In 170 years of unrestricted killing, man all but wiped out the sea otter. By 1911 probably only 1,000 of the animals still existed in all the world. Since then, as a result of international treaties to protect them, otters have now been reestablished in about one fifth of their original coastal range and now number perhaps 130,000. Their survival is a happy episode in the story of conservation.

King and Keeper of the Kelp

The coastal kelp beds, which are the natural habitat of sea otters, are actually the tops of submerged seaweed forests that support rich communities of fish, shellfish and other marine life and, like the canopy of the rain forest, function as a unique world. Sea otters play a significant role in the ecological system of the kelp. They are the only mammals that eat sea urchins, which are gluttonous destroyers of kelp. On the shores of certain Aleutian islands where large colonies of sea otters live, the otters keep the sea urchin populations well under control, and the kelp and kelp-sustained communities of marine life flourish. On neighboring islands where the otters have disappeared, the sea urchins abound, the kelp beds are skimpy and the dependent marine life has been reduced drastically.

In other areas of their range, sea otters are accused of playing a destructive role. California abalone fishermen claim that otters have had an adverse effect on the ecosystem, depleting the shellfish population as efficiently as they have killed off the sea urchins, bringing the shellfish to the brink of extinction. Many conservationists, however, feel that the claims of the fishermen, who themselves take abalone by the ton, are greatly exaggerated.

The kelp bed also functions as a cradle, where mother otters can leave their babies safely while they dive for food. At all other times a female otter and her suckling baby are inseparable, like the seven-week-old youngster and its mother above.

The otters gather in the kelp in colonies of females and pups (above). Males usually live separately, visiting the females only to breed, an act that may occur at any time of the year. The kelp provides a hunting preserve, a playground where the otters frolic and play games, a trysting place and a snug harbor, safe from winds and water currents. Otters rarely venture more than half a mile out to sea, and when they sleep in their kelp beds (right) they usually wrap a few strands of the firmly rooted kelp around their bodies like safety belts to keep from drifting out to sea.

Bon Appétit!

Unlike all other seagoing mammals, sea otters do not have a layer of blubber to keep them warm and, therefore, have an insatiable need for food in order to survive in the cold water, consuming as much as 25 percent of their body weight each day. Having gathered a supply of food, an otter floats supine on the kelp bed, with its chest serving as a breakfast tray. To eat, otters employ their busy forepaws, perhaps a rock, to break a crab shell, or its strong canine teeth to shuck a stubborn clam. Every few minutes during a meal an otter fastidiously turns over in the water to wash the litter from its fur. Keeping its coat immaculate is as important to a sea otter as keeping its belly full. If the fur should become fouled with dirt, it loses its heat-insulating quality, allowing water to penetrate to the skin, and the otter may become chilled and die. Consequently, otters spend over 10 percent of their time grooming themselves.

Having a leisurely meal of kelp crab (left) or clam (above), a sea otter is the picture of relaxed contentment. The coarse mustache is believed to be an aid in locating prey in the murky sea bottom, much as a cat's whiskers help it steer clear of obstacles at night.

With a large "anvil" stone on its chest, a sea otter, one of the world's few tool-using animals, expertly smashes a clamshell to get at the succulent meat. To open many of the mollusks and shellfish it eats, an otter employs rocks or stones, but for one of its favorite foods, the spiny sea urchin, a sea otter needs its paws and strong blunt teeth (overleaf).

Lives of Game Animals

by Ernest Thompson Seton

The prototypal mermaid is said to have been the manatee, but other sea creatures—including certain seals (see page 80)—have also been suggested as the original models for the legendary sirens. In Lives of Game Animals, *Ernest Thompson Seton makes a charming case for the sea otter.*

Like all sea mammals, the otters were originally creatures of the land, but Seton, a prolific recorder of natural history, makes it clear that the frolicsome otters have found a world of their own in the hospitable kelp beds at the edge of the sea.

Of all the creatures living in the cold North seas, the Sea-otter is alone in that he usually swims on his back. Sailing, paddling, shooting or diving he goes, with his back to the deep, and his shining breast to the sky. But his neck is doublebent, so his big soft eyes sweep the blue world above and around. Propelled almost wholly by his big finlike hind feet, he moves with easy sinuous sweeps through the swell with its huge broad fronds of kelp— with back first, he ever goes forward, until the moment comes to dive—supple as an eel he turns—back up like Seal or Beaver, and down he goes—down, down—long strings of silver bubbles mark the course, and by a strange atmospheric change, the colour of the black merman now is yellow-brown as a seaman's slicker, or golden as a bunch of kelp. Down 30 to 100 feet or more he goes, and gropes around in the gloom, until he finds some big fat squid or sea-urchin. He does not hurry, for he can stay under 4 or 5 minutes. Then up he comes with the prey in his jaws, back to the top, to the borderland, that eternal line between the two kingdoms of air and water, on which he lives.

Here again on his back he lies, as, using his broad chest for dinner table, he tears open the sea beastie, feeds on its meat, and flings its shell aside, if it have any. Then he repeats the dive, and the feasting, until his sleek round belly is well filled. Now, among the heaving, friendly kelp he lazes on his back, plays ball perhaps with a lump of the leathery weed, tossing it from paw to paw, taking keen delight in his cleverness at keeping it aloft, as a juggler

does his balls; and sniffing in disappointment if he should foozle the ball and miss the catch.

Other Sea-otters are about him, for Amikuk, like most fishermen, is of a neighbourly spirit and loves good company. His mate may be there with her water baby in her big motherly lap. She tumbles it off into the deep for a swimming lesson; and round and under she swims to exercise "the kid," and make it learn. This is a very ancient game, this water-tag; the earliest monad that ever wriggled tail in the hot first seas, no doubt invented it. It is deep in everything that swims, or moves, and loves good company; so father Otter pitches in, and plays it, too. For half an hour they may keep it up. Father is still strong and frolicsome; so is mother; but the water baby is tired. Its big round eyes are blinking in weariness, and it is ready for sleep. Trust mother to look out for the little one. She curls up and takes it, not pick-a-back, but in the snug bed she makes by curling belly up, as she floats among the weed. Her four feet are the bedposts, and in some degree the coverlet, too, for she holds it to her breast, crooning softly to it, till its whimpering ceases and it sleeps. Its fur may be

wet and cold, but its skin is dry and warm; and drifting like a log of drift among that helpful wrack, they float, and love the lives they live.

But father is full of energy. He is one of thirty or forty that herd along this bed of kelp, that marks a deep-down feeding ridge, where their shiny seafood swarms. And away they go, in a race that recalls the tremendous speed and energy of the Porpoise in the sea. Undulating like water serpents, or breaking from the side of a billow, to leap in a long curve, splash into the high wet bank of the next; one after another they go, racing round, in air or far below, diving, jumping, plunging, somersaulting, back up, belly up, or sides up—it matters not, so they speed, for the joy of rapid flight, for the wonderful pleasure of using their pent-up energy in mastery of the elements about them.

Strange as it may seem, these merry games have mostly place in rough and heavy weather, almost a storm. Swanson says that, on calmer days, they are never seen playing; that is, the bands of older ones are not. They need the stimulus of a contest with the waves before they do their wonderful best. In quiet times, they are more likely to sleep. . . .

As they float their merman way, they are frequently seen with hind flippers raised and spread, as if catching the breeze to sail or drift before it.

On sunny days, so rare in their wild, stormy ocean home, their big brown eyes might suffer from the unwonted glare; but as they float and dream, they sometimes shade their eyes with one idle paw; just as one of us might do, if we could swim that way, and faced the light.

They do not have those big, fawn-like eyes for nothing. Their vision is all it should be, for such perfect organs. Their ears, too, are keen; but of all their senses, smell is their best, the safest sentinel that guards their life.

Best equipped is he, in this respect, of all the wild things in the wild and windy North. But also hardest pressed. For that matchless robe, worth its weight in gold, has the force of a blood-price on his head. Many a brave and valiant man has been hunted down for less reward than the fetch of this wondrous pelt. . . .

And as one reads of its mild and human face, its fish-like hinder parts, its human arms, in which the mother, two-breasted, carries her whimpering babe, and croons it to its slumber, or plays with it, as she sports in the rolling surf, can one not readily believe that in this we have, perhaps, the original of the mermaids and mermen of the ancient tales?

Songs and Sounds from the Deep

Since early Greco-Roman times it has been known that dolphins and porpoises possess an exceptionally keen sense of hearing. Aristotle observed that dolphin-hunters used loud noises to drive their prey ashore, noting that "even a small noise . . . sounds very heavy and enormous to anything which can hear under water." He puzzled over the fact that "the dolphin has the power of hearing but no ears" and observed that the dolphin could make sounds as well as hear them: "When taken out of water [it] gives a squeak and moans." Later investigators discovered that whales—the smaller, toothed species in particular—have elaborate, highly developed auditory systems that do not depend on external ears for their efficiency.

It was not until the present century that scientists began to find out just how exceptional the dolphin's auditory system is. One spur to the scientific investigation of the dolphin was the U.S. Navy's long search for a device for detecting enemy submarines and for guiding undersea craft past obstacles and toward targets. By the end of World War II, a primitive version of sonar (for sound navigation and ranging) was in operation. Sonar is a system which involves the sending and receiving of sound waves and the

Using its sonar to find its target, a blindfolded dolphin at Hawaii's Sea Life Park successfully pierces a ring with its beak.

measuring of the length of time the waves take between going out and coming back. If they strike an object within their range, the returned echo can give a trained operator an accurate notion of the size, shape and distance of the object.

The connection between sonar and sea mammal performance was close; in fact, sonar's developers had used information about these and other echolocating animals such as bats in their research. It was reasonable to suppose that the whales and delphinids must have an echolocating sense because they are able to move very fast under water (as fast as 30 miles per hour) without crashing into foreign objects. Since it was known that whales had a weak sense of smell, and it was clear that their eyes were not of much use in the dark and turbid underwater world, it was theorized that some substitute sense must be used both for navigation and for finding food.

In 1951 Dr. Winthrop N. Kellogg, then Professor of Experimental Psychology at Florida State University, began a series of experiments that proved beyond all doubt that dolphins had a sophisticated, built-in sonar system that made the U.S. Navy's seem positively primitive. Wrote Kellogg: "The underwater sounds which porpoises produce most often are successive series of rapidly repeated clicks or pings [that were] found to contain a wide band of both sonic and ultrasonic frequencies extending as high as 170,000 cycles per second. . . . The ear and brain of the animal have been shown to be highly advanced in development." In short, Kellogg concluded, dolphins are endowed with "an acute transmitting-receiving mechanism" that permits them to "see" by sound waves. Kellogg and his fellow scientists tried every trick they could devise to test a dolphin—blindfolding it, hiding its food in dye-darkened pools, placing artificial barriers in front of its target. In every case the animal zeroed in on the object of its quest with ease.

It was also discovered that dolphins can differentiate between plates of various kinds of metals or of different thicknesses. The Navy has experimented with this ability, with the objective of training dolphins to distinguish underwater mines from harmless scrap metal and to mark their location. A bottle-nosed dolphin learned to tell the difference between a two-and-one-half- and a two-and-one-eighth-inch ball while blindfolded.

This ability of dolphins to "see," as described by Dr.

In a demonstration of how dolphins might be useful to man in his forays beneath the sea, a bottlenose at Sea Life Park in Hawaii, toting a reserve tank of air, comes to the aid of a diver.

Although not considered as bright as porpoises and dolphins, seals, such as Gimpy, the five-year-old sea lion above, have been trained to execute a number of maneuvers. For example, the sound of a buzzer sends Gimpy diving to the bottom of his tank to retrieve a wrench from his trainer.

Peter Warshall, an animal behaviorist, in the anthology *Mind in the Waters*, can be likened to a sort of nonvisual X ray: "If a human diver jumps into the water with a dolphin, the dolphin can 'see' inside the diver into the air passages of his lungs and respiratory system. This is because sonar sight penetrates materials that are approximately the same density as the water—like human flesh—and returns different echoes from objects with different densities. The greater the differences in density, the more easily sonar can discriminate. In the case of the diver, his lungs show a greater contrast to the water than his wet suit."

Formidable as such abilities are, they do not match the powers attributed to dolphins by another pioneer in cetacean research. Dr. John C. Lilly, a distinguished but controversial neurophysiologist, believes that dolphins can communicate by sound, or "talk." Lilly became in-

112

volved in lengthy cetacean research almost by accident when he joined a team of fellow brain specialists in a 1955 project at Florida's Marineland Research Laboratories. The group planned to map a bottle-nosed dolphin's cerebral cortex and ascertain as far as possible the functions of its various parts.

Lilly and his colleagues had done the same experiment on land mammals and regarded the surgical procedures as routine. But they had not counted on the problems inherent in anesthetizing a cetacean, which, instead of inhaling and exhaling regularly, takes in a breath and holds it. When the Lilly group administered anesthesia to their first dolphin, it relaxed, let all of the air out of its lungs and never breathed again. Repeated attempts to render a bottlenose unconscious while keeping it alive failed. Dr. Lilly became so interested in the problem that he worked out a method of using a local anesthetic to implant electrodes in the dolphin's brain with which he stimulated various parts of the dolphin's cortex.

The results were so startling that when Dr. Lilly presented them in a scientific paper at a San Francisco meeting, he became the center of a controversy that has yet to subside. All marine biologists accept the proposition that the dolphin and other cetaceans use their sound-emitting powers not only for echolocating but also for communication with others of their species. Lilly's conclusions went far beyond that. His electrodes, introduced into what he called "negative" and "positive" zones of the animal's brain, produced what he reported as distinct vocalizations of the stimulated emotions: a high, thin "distress whistle" when the negative zone was stimulated and "a large repertory of assorted complex whistles, Bronx cheers and impolite noises" indicating sheer joy when the positive zone was tickled electronically. The porpoise almost immediately learned how to use its beak to turn on the switch controlling the positive-zone stimulus.

This was not especially astounding. The same experiments had been carried out on monkeys, with similar results. But Lilly went further. He reported that when the electricity was cut off so that the bottlenose could not turn on the happiness-making electrode it vocalized its objections in no uncertain terms. Lilly told his scientific audience that one time the dolphin had made some very peculiar sounds on tape. It "had been mimicking some of the things I had been saying. . . . He also reproduced our laughter in a fairly accurate way." This experience convinced Lilly that it was possible for man and dolphin to establish meaningful, articulate communication, either by man learning to interpret the delphinid whistles, squeaks, squawks and blats—or by teaching dolphins to speak English.

Though the matter of delphinid powers of speech remains a controversy, all cetologists agree that some of the large whales sing. From early whaling days it was known that the great creatures made noises; they were so noisy, in fact, that their sounds were sometimes audible through the hulls of whaling vessels. For years scientists have agreed that the vocalizations were part of the whales' echolocation system, designed to locate their prey in the great depths where they hunt. But a series of studies has revealed that some whale noises are actually melodic songs in fixed patterns that are repeated almost like bird songs but are longer and musically more complicated.

Since 1952 recordings of the sounds and songs of 25 species of whales have been made, and cetologists have concluded that the humpback is probably the most vocal and has the most varied musical repertory. For more than 10 years cetologists Roger S. Payne and Frank Watlington have taped the sound of a herd of wintering humpbacks from a hydrophone installation located at a depth of more than 2,000 feet off Bermuda and have discovered that the songs are as distinct and identifiable as if they had been written by a composer. The shortest aria lasts six minutes, the longest about half an hour. The songs are repeated season after season, the same refrains sung—presumably—by different whales. The singers sometimes reprise their melodies for hours, pausing only to blow off the air from their lungs.

The music of the whales is as mysterious and enchanting as a siren song, and scientists have been unable to interpret the melodies or explain their meaning, if any. Since they are heard most frequently at the time when the humpbacks may be breeding, some cetologists speculate that they might be songs of love.

Research zoologist Roger Payne (above, right) and an assistant (left) look on as his wife, Katy Payne (center), unravels hydrophonic equipment in the waters off the coast of Argentina—a favorite wintering spot for right whales—to pick up the sounds made by these colossal 55-foot creatures.

Struggle for Survival

It is surely a cruel paradox that of all the world's wild creatures, none have been more extensively hunted and systematically slaughtered than the seagoing mammals. Most of them are harmless, intelligent and naturally predisposed to friendship with man. But, because they are endowed with attributes of great commercial value—the sleek fur of the sea otter, the ivory of the tusked walrus, the oil-producing blubber of the whale—they are in peril, for the harvesting of such rich prizes requires the animals' death. Man has killed them by the millions. And wherever he has hunted, man has depicted these endeavors in his art,

a selection of which is shown here and on the following pages. In recent years the wisdom and morality of such slaughter has been a subject of debate, and there are signs of a consensus for calling a halt to the killing before the cetaceans, sirenians, pinnipeds and marine mustelids disappear altogether.

The so-called great whales—comprising nine or ten species—have suffered most from man's encroachments, for it is they who over the years have individually and collectively provided the greatest profits. Whale hunting probably started with the Norwegians as far back as the first

This detailed painting of a dolphin was executed more than 3,000 years ago on the rock wall of a cave in northern Australia.

114

An 18th century painting by A. V. Salm, a prolific seascape artist, depicts the intensive Dutch whaling activity at the time.

century B.C. Little is known of the Norwegians' methods or the extent of their catches. The invention of modern whaling is generally credited to another adventurous and enterprising people, the Basques of southern France and northern Spain. Sometime around the 11th or 12th centuries A.D. they began to cut up beached whales and boil their blubber into oil for lighting and heating and to use their meat for food. Later, these hardy inhabitants of the rugged coasts of the Bay of Biscay sent out fleets of small boats to herd the cetaceans into shallow water, where they could be killed with long lances that the hunters called "harpoons." By the beginning of the 16th century the Basques had discovered that whale oil and other products were much desired by other peoples and could serve as a valuable item of trade. So, the organized whaling industry began. They built larger ships, 70-foot caravels of 50- to 60-ton capacity, in which they sailed across the Atlantic to

Newfoundland and eventually wandered as far as the Arctic Ocean in search of the Greenland right whale. The Basques initiated the practice of flensing, or stripping, the blubber and rendering it into oil by boiling it in shipboard pots on fires fueled by whale oil. (This was an efficient but dangerous procedure, for if the oil spilled, the whole ship could be burned in a matter of minutes.)

In the 17th century the Dutch and British entered the whaling business, and by 1680 the Dutch had 260 whalers with a total crew of 14,000 going to the Arctic, all carrying experienced Basque harpooners and flensers. During the next 200 years the British and Dutch had exterminated most of the bowhead whales in the northern hemisphere; the species never fully recovered from this early slaughter. On the other side of the world the Japanese had independently started their own whaling industry, going after the gray, the right, the humpback, the sei and even the elusive

115

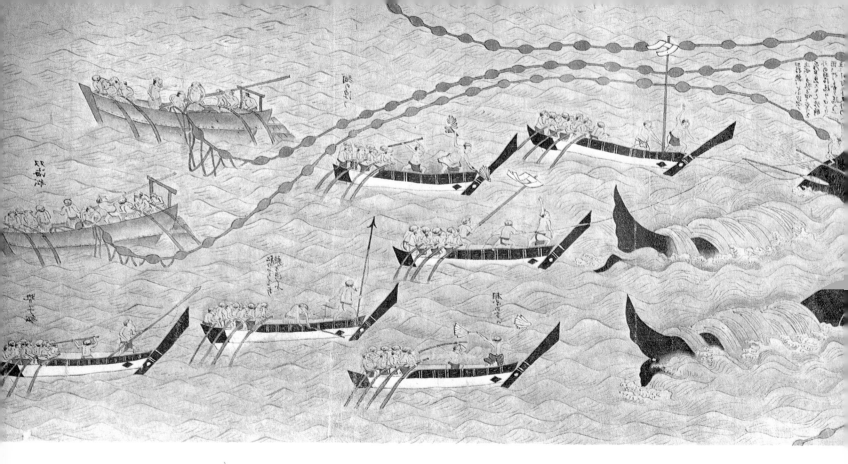

Early whaling techniques are illustrated in this Japanese watercolor scroll taken from a book written in 1773.

sperm whale.

In America the Indians had used small boats to hunt the humpback and the right whale in the shallow waters off New England long before the coming of the European settlers. At first the new Americans copied the Indians' tactics, but soon they built larger ships and sailed beyond the sight of land in search of their quarry. In 1712 Captain Christopher Hussey, hunting right whales out of Nantucket, managed to kill a sperm whale and bring it back with its extremely valuable spermaceti as well as the blubber. His success prompted enterprising New Englanders to build still larger ships to harvest the wide-ranging but more profitable sperm, and thus the American sperm whaling industry was born. By the end of the century sailing ships were traveling out of Nantucket and New Bedford as far south as Cape Horn in search of the sperm whale, and in the mid-19th century, when the industry reached its zenith, there were more than 700 American whalers roaming most of the seas of the world. The only circumstance that restricted the slaughter was the fact that the relatively slow sailing ships were capable of only limited catches.

For similar reasons the giant rorquals were relatively safe from the whalers until the advent of steam, for the animals swam too fast to be pursued under sail and were too big to be approached in small boats. Just as steam eventually gave more speed to the hunters, another invention foreshadowed the doom of even the biggest and swiftest of the cetaceans: In 1864, Svend Foyn, a Norwegian skipper, invented the harpoon gun with an explosive head, which allowed whalers to shoot their quarry from a distance. Further technological innovations combined to turn what was already heavy killing into a production-line massacre. These were procedures for pumping air into harpooned whales to keep them from sinking the moment they die, as rorquals do, and the development of the modern factory ship for processing whale products at sea on a newly efficient basis. By 1910 there were almost no whales left in the northern hemisphere, and by the 1920s the big factory ships steamed into the Antarctic in great numbers.

Faced with the massive reduction of whale pods, the commercial whaling nations met in Geneva in 1931 and signed the International Convention for the Regulation of Whaling. Ratified by the U.S. Senate in 1935, the treaty protected right whales and bowheads, already commer-

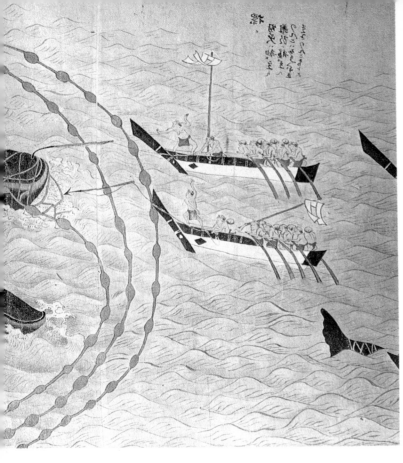

This engraving, done in 1744, depicts whalemen in Spitsbergen and shows some of the equipment that was used to haul the huge creatures ashore.

A Whale Female and the Windlais whereby the Whales are brought on shore

The pages at right are taken from the logbook of the whaler Mary and Susan. The left-hand page details the whaling signals used and shows, through drawings, the whales that got away. The right-hand page depicts successful catches.

Until the invention of modern whaling equipment many seamen lost their lives in battles with whales. The painting below, done in 1877, by an American artist, shows a small whaling boat broken in half by the powerful thrash of a whale's flukes.

This illustration from a 19th-century manuscript depicts an Arctic expedition in search of walruses.

cially extinct, and forbade the killing of females with calves. The slaughter of other species continued unabated, however, and in 1946 a new international body was established, the International Whaling Commission, in which 16 whaling nations are now represented. But the IWC, torn by controversy and hampered by greed and national self-interest, has had a troubled history. The IWC, which continued to protect the right and bowhead whales, added the gray whale in 1946. It has, however, been very slow in agreeing on protective measures for other species. In 1962—16 years after the establishment of the commission —the whaling industry posted an all-time record slaughter of 66,090 whales. That same year the IWC admitted its failure to restrict the killing of the great blue by reporting that the world population of the leviathan had been re-

duced by an estimated nine tenths since 1946. The catch figures for 1964 are a practical example of this ninefold decimation: Out of a total world take of 63,001 whales, only 372 were blues, compared with the 43,130 whales killed during the 1930–1931 season, out of which 29,649 were blues. Faced with these grim statistics, the quarreling members of the IWC finally agreed in 1966 to place a total ban on the killing of the blue, which has been reduced to an estimated total population of 12,000. Since then, in the face of opposition—and outright defiance—from Japan and the Soviet Union, the IWC has added the humpback and the fin whale to the list of totally prohibited species and has set whaling quotas for all other species.

As of 1972 it was illegal for U.S. citizens either to engage in the whaling industry or to import whale products into

Off Greenland, 19th century hunters pursue whales from boats and take to the floes to hunt seals and small aquatic birds.

the country. (The United States Marine Mammals Act of 1972 extended the ban to include all marine mammals.) The U.S. also took the lead in advocating a worldwide cessation of all commercial whaling and in the same year proposed a 10-year moratorium on the killing of whales. The moratorium was approved by a vote of 53 to 0 by the United Nations Conference on the Human Environment. But in the IWC, the United States has repeatedly failed to obtain the necessary three-fourths majority to implement the proposed moratorium. Although the IWC has passed selective moratoriums on various species in different parts of the world, many conservationists are highly doubtful that the international body will act fast enough to save the remaining great whales of the world from extinction. The only hope seems to be that, as each species is reduced to a

number that makes continued commercial hunting unprofitable, it will be left alone; but that is a frail hope, since species cannot survive unless they exist in sufficient numbers to overcome the natural perils of their habitat and locate each other.

Although the United States may be justifiably proud of its record on whale conservation, it should be very concerned with the plight of dolphins. Even though they are legally protected, dolphins present a special problem: their close association with the yellowfin tuna, of which U.S. fishermen take millions of pounds annually. Nobody knows why the bottle-nosed, the spotted, the spinner and common dolphin, among other delphinids, join schools of tuna, especially favoring the yellowfin. Until the late 1950s their fraternity posed no difficulty. Tuna fishermen would watch for dolphins swimming on the surface above great schools of tuna, "chum up" the tuna by throwing bait into the water, put over their hooked lines and haul in the fish, thankful to the dolphins for showing them where the tuna were.

In recent years, however, the tuna fishing industry has replaced lines with huge nets to haul in their catches. As a result, the dolphins get caught with the tuna in the nets. Unable to get free to surface and breathe, the mammals suffocate. Director Robert W. Schoning of the National Marine Fisheries Service recently testified before a Congressional committee that in 1971 an estimated 300,000 dolphins were "incidentally" killed in tuna nets. As a result of public outrage the toll dropped to 134,000 in 1975, and 1976 losses were estimated at fewer than 78,000. But anxious conservationists insist that the figure is still too high, and further legislation is pending.

North Pacific fur seals, which have been protected by

Two Aleut Indians, Alaskans who are highly skilled at hunting sea mammals, prepare to kill a sea otter in this watercolor.

Modern whale-hunting techniques include the harpoon gun with exploding head, seen here aboard a "killer boat" off South Africa.

treaties between the United States, Russia, Japan and Canada since 1911, are facing different problems. Protection of the seals, chief providers of sealskin coats, has resulted in their increasing numbers on the Pribilof and Commander islands. Although some observers contend that their populations have increased to the extent that some are dying from disease, overcrowding and starvation, most environmentalists strongly dispute this theory of "overpopulation." They believe that the seals should be left alone and question the concept that man can do a better job of keeping animals healthy than can nature.

Among other members of the pinniped family, a few species, notably the walrus, have been hunted to near extinction. As for the sirenians, both the manatee and the dugong are on the U.S. list of endangered species, but little is being done on an international level to assure their survival. As a result of the 1911 treaty, however, the smallest of the aquatic mammals, the four-foot sea otter, seems to be flourishing once more in its California and North Pacific coastal habitats.

Viewed against this background, the world's performance in the preservation of the sea mammals must be ranked poor, despite some recent steps in the right direction. This situation is paradoxical, however, particularly in the case of great whales, whose aura of majesty (overleaf) speaks to the best human instincts and calls forth the most profound sense of kinship between man and his fellow animals.

Flensers, who strip the blubber from whales, work over a rorqual aboard a Japanese whaling ship.

Credits

Cover—Bruce Coleman, Inc. 1—J. Rychetnik from Photo Researchers, Inc. 5—Paul Chesley. 6—W. Curtsinger from Photo Researchers, Inc. 7—(top) John Dominis, Time, Inc., (bottom) W. Ruth, Bruce Coleman, Inc. 9—F. Lyon from Rapho Division, Photo Researchers, Inc. 15—D. Cavagnaro, Time, Inc. 17, 18, 20–21, 22–23—Jen and Des Bartlett from Bruce Coleman, Inc. 23—(top,left) K. Read from Sea Library, (top, right) A. Giddings from Sea Library, (middle) Tom Stack & Assoc. from Sea Library, (bottom) Tom Stack & Assoc. from Sea Library. 24–25—Russ Kinne from Photo Researchers, Inc. 28, 29—L. Cochrane from Sea Library. 30, 31, 32–33—John Dominis, Time, Inc. 42—Ken Balcomb from Sea Library. 43 (top)—Russ Kinne from Photo Researchers, Inc., (bottom) Bruce Coleman, Inc. 44—(top) Tom McHugh for Marineland from Photo Researchers, Inc. 44–45—John Molholm. 47—Russ Kinne from Photo Researchers, Inc. 48—Photo Researchers, Inc. 49—Nina Leen, Time, Inc. 52–53—Jen and Des Bartlett from Bruce Coleman, Inc. 54, 55—D. Caldwell, Biological Systems, Inc. 56—Bruce Coleman, Inc. 57, 58—Jen and Des Bartlett from Bruce Coleman, Inc. 59—R. Hernandez from Photo Researchers, Inc. 63—J. Powell. 64—(top) Russ Kinne from Photo Researchers, Inc., (bottom)—Peter Murray Hart, N. Y. Aquarium. 65—Ron Church/Tom Stack & Associates. 67—A. Power from Bruce Coleman, Inc. 71, 72, 73—Jen and Des Bartlett from Bruce Coleman, Inc. 74—Thase Daniels. 75—(left) G. Harrison from Bruce Coleman, Inc., (right) Bruce Coleman, Inc. 76—(top) C. Roessler from Sea Library, (bottom) D. B. Westfall from Sea Library. 77—(top) D. B. Westfall from Sea Library, (bottom) C. Roessler from Sea Library. 78—J. Rychetnik from Photo Researchers, Inc. 79—(left) Bruce Coleman, Inc., (right) R. Hernandez from Photo Researchers, Inc. 81—S. Leatherwood from Sea Library. 82—(top and bottom) R. Hernandez from Photo Researchers, Inc. 83—(top) C. Ray from Photo Researchers, Inc., (bottom) G. Holton from Photo Researchers, Inc. 84—(left and right) Thase Daniels. 85—(left) T. McHugh for Pt. Defiance Zoo, Photo Researchers, Inc., (right) C. Ray from Photo Researchers, Inc. 86—Jen and Des Bartlett from Bruce Coleman, Inc. 88–89—B. Evans from Sea Library. 89—Jen and Des Bartlett from Bruce Coleman, Inc. 90—R. Hernandez from Photo Researchers, Inc. 90–91—B. Evans from Sea Library. 92—G. Holton from Photo Researchers, Inc. 93—(top) W. Curtsinger from Rapho Division, Photo Researchers, Inc., (bottom) G. Holton from Photo Researchers, Inc. 94–95—N. K. Temnikow from Sea Library. 96—Fritz Gro, Time, Inc. 97—A. Giddings from Sea Library. 98—Thau/Zefa. 99—(left) C. Ray from Photo Researchers, Inc., (right)—G. Holton from Photo Researchers, Inc. 101, 102, 103, 104, 105—J. Foott from Bruce Coleman, Inc. 106–107—Scott Ransom. 110—Jen and Des Bartlett from Bruce Coleman, Inc. 111—H. Groskinsky, Time, Inc. 112—Flip Schulke, Black Star. 113—W. Curtsinger from Photo Researchers, Inc. 114—G. Gerster from Rapho Division, Photo Researchers, Inc. 122—Peter Lake, Sea Library. 123—Hiroshi Yagishita. 124–125—W. Curtsinger. 128—J. Rychetnik from Photo Researchers, Inc.

Photographs on endpapers are used courtesy of Time-Life Picture Agency, Russ Kinne and Stephen Dalton of Photo Researchers, Inc. and Nina Leen.

Film sequences on pages 8 and 14 are from "Sea of Cortez," the sequence on page 45 is from the "The Living Arctic" and the frame on page 87 is from "Elephant Seals," programs in the Time-Life Television series Wild, Wild World of Animals.

MAP on page 66 is by Enid Kotschnig.

ILLUSTRATION on pages 10–11 is courtesy of the National Marine Fisheries Service, National Oceanic and Atmospheric Administration, U. S. Department of Commerce, artist Rod Ruth; those on pages 12 and 13 are by Enid Kotschnig. The paintings on pages 19, 26–27 and 41 are by Richard Ellis, and the painting on page 48 is by George Luther Schelling. The illustrations on pages 34, 35, 37 and 39 are courtesy of the Rockwell Kent legacies and the Weyhe Gallery. The illustration on page 50 is by André Durenceau. The illustrations on pages 60–61 and 108–109 are by John Groth. The illustrations on pages 115, 116 and 118 (bottom) are courtesy of the Kendall Whaling Museum, Sharon, Massachusetts. The illustration on page 117 is courtesy of the New York Public Library. The illustration on page 118 (top) is courtesy of Old Dartmouth Historical Society, Whaling Museum, New Bedford, Massachusetts. The illustration on page 119 is courtesy of Sea Library, photographer P. Thomas. The illustration on page 120 is courtesy of the Mariners Museum, Newport, Virginia. The illustration on page 121 is by Emilie Curtis, photographed by J. Foott from Bruce Coleman, Inc.

Bibliography

Alpers, Antony, Dolphins: The Myth and the Mammal. Houghton Mifflin, 1961.

Bertram, Colin, In Search of Mermaids. Cromwell, 1964.

Caldwell, David, The World of the Bottlenosed Dolphin. Lippincott, 1972.

Cousteau, Jacques-Yves, and Diole, Philippe, Dolphins. Doubleday, 1975.

———, The Whale, Mighty Monarch of the Sea. Doubleday, 1972.

Cromie, William J., The Living World of the Sea. Prentice-Hall, 1966.

Daetz, Gary, Rookery Island. Rand McNally, 1967.

Devine, Elizabeth, and Clark, Martha, The Dolphin Smile. Macmillan, 1967.

Gaskin, D. E., Whales, Dolphins and Seals. Heinemann Educational Books, 1972.

Grzimek, Bernhard, Grzimek's Animal Life Encyclopedia. Van Nostrand Reinhold, 1975.

Hill, David O., "Vanishing Giants." Audubon, January 1975, pp. 56, 92.

*Howell, A. B., Aquatic Mammals, Their Adaptations to Life in the Water. Dover, 1970.

*Kellogg, Winthrop N., Porpoises and Sonar. University of Chicago Press, 1961.

*Kenyon, Karl W., The Sea Otter in the Eastern Pacific Ocean. Dover, 1975.

King, Judith, Seals of the World. British Museum, 1966.

Life Nature Library, The Sea. Time, Inc., 1961, 1972.

*Lilly, John C., Man and Dolphin. Doubleday, 1961.

Lockley, R. M., Grey Seal, Common Seal. October House, 1966.

*McIntyre, Joan, editor, Mind in the Waters. Scribners, 1974.

McNulty, Faith, The Great Whales. Doubleday, 1974.

Matthews, L. Harrison, Sea Elephant. Macgibbon and Kee, et al., 1966

———, The Whale. Crescent, 1974.

Maxwell, Gavin, Seals of the World. Houghton Mifflin, 1967.

*Mowat, Farley, A Whale for the Killing. Little, Brown, 1972.

Nayman, Jacquelin, Whales, Dolphins and Man. Hamlyn Publishing Group, 1973.

Norman, J. R., and Fraser, F. C., Field Book of Giant Fishes, Whales and Dolphins. Putnam, 1937.

Norris, Kenneth, editor, *Whales, Dolphins and Porpoises.* University of California Press, 1966.

Payne, Roger, "Swimming with Patagonia's Right Whales." *National Geographic,* October 1972, p. 577.

———, "At Home with Right Whales." *National Geographic,* March 1976, p. 322.

Perry, Richard, *The Polar Worlds.* Taplinger, 1973.

Pruna, Andres, "Secret Life of the Right Whale." *Audubon,* January 1975, p. 40.

Reiger, George, "Dolphin sacred, porpoise profane." *Audubon,* January 1975, p. 3.

*Scammon, Charles Melville, *The Marine Mammals of the Northwestern Coast of North America.* Dover, 1968.

Scheffer, Victor B., *A Natural History of Marine Mammals.* Scribners, 1976.

*———, *The Year of the Seal.* Scribners, 1970.

———, *Seals, Sea Lions and Walruses: A Review of the Pinnipedia.* Stanford University Press, 1958.

Shor, Franc, editor, *The Marvels of Animal Behavior.* National Geographic Society, 1972.

Slijper, E. J., *Whales.* Basic Books. 1962.

Stenuit, Robert, *The Dolphin, Cousin to Man.* Sterling, 1968.

Time-Life Books, Editors of, *The Vanishing Species.* Time-Life Books, 1974.

Vontobel, Roy, "Diary of a Whaling Voyage." *Audubon,* January 1975, p. 30.

Walker, Ernest P., *et al., Mammals of the World,* Vol. II. Johns Hopkins, 1968.

Wise, William, *The Strange World of Sea Mammals.* Putnam, 1973.

Wood, Forrest G., *Marine Mammals and Man.* Luce, 1973.

Index

Andersen, Hans Christian, 14
Art, sea mammals and, 14
Auks, 13

Baleen whales (Mysticeti), 10–11, 16–39; blowholes of, 42; feeding habits of, 10, 13, 16, 22–23; gray whales, 10–11, 15, 16, 17, 26, 29, 123; hunting of, 16; right whales, 10–11, 13, 16–23; rorquals, 10–11, 16, 24–25, 116; size of, 16
Bearded seal, 83
Beasts of the Sea (Steller), 68–69
Beluga whale. *See* White whale
Blue whale, 10–11, 24–25; hunting of, 16, 119; size of, 16, 24
Bottle-nosed dolphins, 46, 47, 120; intelligence of, 49; reproduction and nursing of young, 54–55
Bowhead whale, 10–11
Bryde's rorqual, 16

Callosities, 19
Cetaceans: evolution of, 8; intelligence of, 14, 49, 56. *See also* Dolphins; Porpoises; Whales, 10–61
Columbus, Christopher, 14, 62
Copepods, 23
Cousteau, Jacques-Yves, 50–52
Crabeater seal, 82

Delphinids. *See* Dolphins; Porpoises
Dolphins, 40, 46–61, 114, 120–121; bottle-nosed, 46, 47, 54–55, 120; common, 46, 120; communication among, 110–113; evolution of, 8; false killer whale, 56–57; feeding habits of, 54, 56, 58–59; intelligence of, 49, 56; killer whale (orca), 46 56, 58–59

Dugongs, 62, 64–65; evolution of, 8, 12; habitat of, 62; near extinction of, 62, 64, 122

Eared seals, 70–81; fur seals, 70, 78–79, 81, 92, 121–122; sea lions, 9, 10–11, 58, 70, 71–77, 92
Elephant seal, 70, 82, 86–91
Ellis, Richard, 19
Euphausia superba, 23
Evolution of sea mammals, 8, 12–13, 62

False killer whale, 56–57
Fin whales, 10–11, 16, 119
Foyn, Svend, 116
Fur seals, 70, 78–79, 81, 92, 121–122

Gray whale, 10–11, 15, 16, 17, 26–29, 115; migration of, 27, 28; playfulness of, 28–29; protection of, 27

Harbor porpoises, 49
Harbor seals, 85
Harp seals, 84
Hudson, Henry, 14
Humpback whale, 10–11, 13, 30–33, 119; playfulness of, 31, 33
Hussey, Captain Christopher, 116

International Convention for the Regulation of Whaling, 116
International Whaling Commission, 24, 30, 119, 120

Kellogg, Dr. Winthrop, 11
Killer whale (orca), 46, 56, 58–59, 92
Krill, 10, 22, 92

Layard's (strap-toothed) whale, 40
Leopard seals, 70, 92–95
Lilly, Dr. John C., 112–113
Literature, sea mammals in, 14, 62
Lives of Game Animals (Seton), 108–109
Living Sea, The (Cousteau), 50–52
Lobtailing, 21

Mammals, basic characteristics of, 8, 13, 62
Man as hunter and enemy of sea mammals, 14, 16, 24, 27, 28, 30, 40, 45, 62, 64, 70, 79, 96, 100, 114–122
Manatees, 10–11, 62–67, 122; evolution of, 8, 12; feeding habits of, 62, 64; habitat of, 62; mating and birth of, 62; skeletal forelimb of, 12
Marine Mammals and Man (Wood), 13
Marine Protection Act of 1972, 10
Melville, Herman, 34–39, 40
Mind in the Waters (Warshall), 112
Minke rorqual, 16
Moby Dick (Melville), 14, 34–39, 40, 42
Monk seals, 84
Music, sea mammals and, 14
Mustelids, 8
Mythology, sea mammals and, 14, 40, 62

Narwhal, 40, 120; tusk of, 40, 45
National Marine Fisheries Service, 121
Natural History of Marine Mammals, A (Scheffer), 8
New York Zoological Society, 18

Payne, Katy, 113
Payne, Dr. Roger, 19, 21, 113
Penguins, 13, 92, 93
Pilot whales, 44–45; skeletal forelimb of, 12

Pinnipeds: evolution of, 8, 12; feeding habits of, 70; mating, birth and care of young, 70, 72–79, 82, 84, 94, 99. *See also* Eared seals; Seals, true; Walruses, 10–11, 70–99, 122

Plenisner, Friedrich, 69

Polar bears, 13

Porpoises, 13, 40, 46–61; common, 46; communication among, 110–113; Dall's, 46

Pteropods, 23

Religion, sea mammals and, 14

Ribbon seal, 83

Right whale, 10–11, 13, 16–23; feeding habits of, 22; Greenland, 18; pygmy, 18; size of, 18; Southern, 17, 18, 20–23; whalers and, 16, 18, 115

Ringed seal, 70, 82, 85

Rorqual family of whales, 10–11, 16, 24–25, 116, 123

Scammon, Charles, 28

Scheffer, Victor B., 8

Schoning, Robert W., 121

Scott, Robert Falcon, 60–61

Scott's Last Expedition (Scott), 60–61

Sea Life Park, Hawaii, 110, 111

Sea lions, 9, 10–11, 58, 70, 71, 92, 112; caring for young, 74–77; courtship and mating, 72–73; habitat of, 75; territoriality of, 72–73

Sea otters, 10–11, 100–109; evolution of, 8, 12; feeding habits of, 100, 102, 104–105; grooming, 104; hunting of, 100, 114, 121; mating, birth and care of young, 100, 103; size of, 100; skeletal forelimb of, 12; social life of, 103

Seafarer's Tale, A, 80

Seals, true (phocids), 10–11, 59, 70, 82–95, 122; child care and, 84, 89; evolution of, 8; feeding habits, 83, 85, 89, 92; molting of, 90–91; skeletal forelimb of, 12

Sei whale, 10–11, 13, 16, 115

Seton, Ernest Thompson, 108–109

Sirenians: evolution of, 8, 12, 62. *See also* Dugongs; Manatees, 62–69, 122

Sperm whale, 10–11, 13, 40, 41, 42, 115–116

Steller, Georg Wilhelm, 62, 68–69, 100

Steller sea cow, 62, 64, 68–69, 100

Toothed whales (Odontoceti), 10–11, 13, 40–61; blowholes of, 42, 43; bottle-nosed and beaked, 40, 46–61, 92; feeding habits of, 10; pilot whale, 12, 44–45; sperm whales, 10–11, 13, 40, 41, 42; white (beluga), 40, 43

Tuna fisherman, 120–121

United Nations Conference on the Human Environment, 120

U.S. endangered species list, 10, 119–120, 122

U.S. Marine Mammals Act of 1972, 120

U.S. Navy, 110, 111

Walruses, 10–11, 70, 71, 96–99, 120; care of young, 99; evolution of, 8; hunting of, 70, 96, 114, 119, 122; tusks of, 70, 96–97, 99

Warshall, Dr. Peter, 111–112

Watlington, Frank, 113

Weddell seals, 59, 70

Whalebone, 22

Whales: baleen, 10–11, 13, 16–39, 42, 123; blows of, 13, 42–43; communication among, 21, 110–113; evolution of, 8; flippers of, 12, 13; flukes of, 20–21, 30, 118; size of, 13; toothed, 10–11, 13, 40–45, 46–61, 92. *See also names of specific whales*, 114–125

Whaling. *See* Man as hunter and enemy of sea mammals

White (beluga) whale, 40, 43

Wood, Forrest G., 13

Zooplankton, 23